ZECHARIAH

Israel's Messenger of the Messiah's Triumph

IN CANADA:

The Christian Friends of Israel Inc
PO Box 51063 Unit 111
25 Peel Centre Dr
Bramalea, Ont. L6T 5M2

ZECHARIAH

Israel's Messenger of the Messiah's Triumph

by Fred H. Hartman

The Friends of Israel Gospel Ministry, Inc.
P. O. Box 908, Bellmawr, NJ 08099

ZECHARIAH: Israel's Messenger of the Messiah's Triumph
©Copyright 1994

The Friends of Israel Gospel Ministry, Inc.

The Friends of Israel Gospel Ministry, Inc.

Acknowledgements

Thisbook would not be in print today without the support and assistance of my faithful co-workers at The Friends of Israel Gospel Ministry, Inc. They constantly encouraged me in the completion of the manuscript, and their faithful labors helped lighten the load. To thank God for them is insufficient. Recognition of their assistance must be made.

A word of thanks goes to Grace Little, my former secretary (now retired), and to Helen Stubbs, my present secretary. They both labored long hours typing and correcting every handwritten word of the manuscript. Elwood McQuaid, our Executive Director, provided guidance and encouragement along the way, and Peter Colón contributed valuable insights.

Amy Julian and our able editorial staff did much to put this volume into its final form.

No one is an entity unto himself. It is only through a team effort that the work of the Lord is accomplished. I thank the Lord for my fellow workers, all faithful servants of the Lord.

Introduction

The Prophet Zechariah's day was a time of deep discouragement for the Jewish people who had returned from the Babylonian captivity. They were so deeply troubled that many had lost their will to continue the daunting task of reclaiming the land. It seemed that God Himself had turned His back on them. The future was so clouded by what appeared to be impending disaster that the national spirit was at a very low ebb. If God was not prepared to intervene, where could they turn?

Eighteen years earlier, this little group of refugees had returned to Jerusalem with hearts overflowing with joy. With a great sense of expectation, they had begun to clear the mass of rubble left from the horrible destruction of the city almost two generations before (587–586 B.C.). Within seven months of their return, the Levitical system of sacrifices had been restored. In the second month of the second year of their return, they had completed the foundations for their new Temple (Ezra 3:8).

Initially, the work went well, and it continued to progress until adversaries conspired to prevent the Jews from completing the work (Ezra 4).

Eighteen years passed during which no construction was done on the Temple, and the people nearly gave up hope of ever rebuilding their place of worship. With their numbers diminished, enemies on every side, and apparently no real leader to guide them, their morale was all but broken. The hardships of nearly two decades of oppression had left them weakened, and their only comfort lay in the thought that at least they were home. Huddled below Jerusalem in the valleys to the south, they waited for someone to come to the fore and restore their hope.

Questions about God's faithfulness haunted them: Had they returned to their land in vain? Why was their God silent? Had He forgotten them? Would He keep His word?

It was at this point that God raised up two prophets with a message for the disheartened remnant. First to appear was the Prophet Haggai. Apparently he was an old man who had seen Solomon's Temple before its destruction, as well as the years of exile endured by Judah. His words were harsh, virtually lashing these Jewish refugees with a message that was short and laced with severe rebuke: "Consider your ways" (Hag. 1:5), he cried. "Is it time for you, O ye, to dwell in your paneled houses, and this house [the Temple] to lie waste? . . . Consider your ways. Go up to the mountain, and bring wood, and build the house" (Hag. 1:4, 7-8). Haggai charged them to go to Mount Moriah and rebuild their Temple, along with the city and its walls. The prophet's words implied that more progress had been made on their personal dwellings than on anything pertaining to the city or sanctuary.

With the thundering speech that only a true prophet of God had the right to use, Haggai poured out his soul to these discouraged and disobedient sons of Abraham, Isaac, and Jacob. Although his messages were of little comfort to a people who had already faced many trials and difficulties, he did reveal that the Lord was with them after all, and the Temple would, in fact, be built. After a ministry of only three months, he left the scene as rapidly as he had arrived.

Two months after Haggai began his brief ministry, the Lord raised up the Prophet Zechariah, a young man who continued to proclaim God's message for many years. Zechariah's message carried a different tone, and his words touched the hearts and lives of this confused band, bringing them hope and encouragement. The very name *Zechariah* means *God remembers*, a reminder they sorely needed at that moment. Even as his message met the immediate need of the returned Jerusalemites, it went far beyond the immediate context to encompass the ages and give an enduring message of hope to troubled people across the centuries. Of even greater significance is the fact that this *minor prophet* delivered a *major message*, the essence of which portrays the glorious prophetic future of Jerusalem and end-time events.

By means of God-given visions, Zechariah transmitted prophecies of the Messiah's two comings. Throughout the book the Messiah is portrayed. He appears in several visions in chapters 1 to 8, and in chapters 9 to 11 He is portrayed as a rejected and crucified leader. Finally, in chapters 12 to 14 He provides cleansing and victory.

Zechariah also proclaimed God's future plans for the Jewish people and Jerusalem. As we have seen, at the time of his prophecy, the nation needed assurances that God had not forsaken them, that He was still deeply concerned about His people.

In a nutshell, the Lord gave Zechariah a message of comfort for hurting Israel. His people would learn that He was on their side and that He intended to bless them and assure the fulfillment of Israel's future destiny.

So, as we shall discover, God had not forgotten His people. Indeed, He had remembered them in a far greater way than they could ever have envisioned, and the good news given in these brief chapters of prophecy would sweep away the bitter memories of the Babylonian captivity. As a matter of fact, Zechariah's prophetic passages surpass in detail and clarity those of many of his Old Testament peers.

My purpose in writing is to explore with you the *major message* of this *minor prophet* in the hope that this little book will significantly impact your life. Pray that, as we study together, the same Holy Spirit who gave the message to Zechariah will work in the innermost recesses of our hearts as well.

ZECHARIAH 1

Background, Visions One and Two

The Characters of the Book

To better comprehend the thrust of the Book of Zechariah, we first must know something about the principle characters. Having been introduced to them, we will better understand how and why Zechariah's prophecy is so powerful. Furthermore, we will discover why Zechariah's prophecy also speaks to many relevant issues in our own lives more than 2,500 years later.

Messiah

The first character of this book is the Messiah. Within these few pages, we see Him in visions as well as in prophecy. Allusions to His person, work, and future glorious reign abound throughout the Book of Zechariah.

An intriguing panorama of His life is portrayed in only 211 verses. Included are His dramatic entrance into Jerusalem on what we call Palm Sunday; His rejection and crucifixion; His Second Coming in glory; and His final acceptance by the nation of Israel. The capstone is the revelation of the future of Jerusalem as the Messiah reigns over it and rules all the nations during the future Millennium.

The key to unlocking the truth contained in Zechariah is the Messiah Jesus. It is therefore understandable that Jewish writers are puzzled over much of the book's content. Believers, however, such as George L. Robinson, describe Zechariah as "the most messianic, the most truly apocalyptic and eschatological of all writings of the Old Testament."[1]

Darius

The book begins, "In the eighth month, in the second year of Darius, . . . " To understand the remainder of the book, it is important to know something about this historical figure. Darius was a Persian king, the second ruler of Persia after the death of Cyrus the Great. Cyrus was the king who had decreed that the Jewish people could return to their homeland following the Babylonian captivity. Cyrus' decree to allow the Jews to return was not unusual for Persian kings. They often allowed conquered people to remain in their homeland and even granted freedom to practice national religions. Consequently, Darius allowed the Jews to live fairly peacefully during his reign.

Zechariah

Zechariah was a common name in the Scriptures. Twenty-seven people were called by this name, so we must take care that we identify the correct one. Zechariah means *whom the Lord remembers* or just *God remembers*, which is certainly the theme of this book and helps explain why so many would employ the name.

In the first verse of the book, Zechariah carefully identified himself as the son of Berechiah and the grandson of Iddo. Why, then, was he called the son of Iddo in Ezra 6:14? Ezra did not mention his father Berechiah possibly because he died young. Perhaps Zechariah was raised by Iddo the priest. Also, skipping a generation was not unusual in the genealogies listed in the Word of God. Iddo was probably one of the priests who returned from captivity in Babylon along with Zerubbabel. Because Zechariah was descended from his priestly line, he was a priest as well as a prophet.

The Challenge of the Past

The challenge of Zechariah to the returning captives was through "the word of the LORD" (v. 1). His first message to the returned exiles was that they were not to live as had their fathers. God's anger with the preceding generation warned them about following a like path. The preexilic prophets had come upon the scene one after another, crying, "Repent, and turn from your evil ways." But the people refused to hear. Therefore, God repeatedly reminded the following generations that if their fathers had obeyed the earlier prophets, they would not have been forced into 70 years of captivity in Babylon, nor would they have known the destruction of their glorious city and Solomon's magnificent Temple. Had they repented, God would have been willing to turn His wrath away and spare the city, just as He had spared a repentant Nineveh in the days of Jonah more than 200 years before. Once again He extended His mercy to them. "Turn unto me," He implored, "and I will turn unto you" (1:3).

The Cry of the Prophet

Just as their forefathers did not listen to God, Zechariah's generation likewise turned away from Him. "Turn now from your evil ways, and from your evil doings," He cried out to the returned exiles (1:4). Zechariah's contemporary, Haggai, was also saying, "Consider your ways" (Hag. 1:5, 7). "Is it time for you, O ye, to dwell in your paneled houses, and this house [the Temple] to lie waste?" (Hag. 1:4). From the mouths of both prophets came one clear and consistent message: Turn back to the Lord.

As recorded in the first chapter of Haggai, when the Jews ran into problems in obeying God's command to rebuild the Temple, they turned to satisfying their own desires and built lovely homes for themselves. As a result, the construction and completion of the house of God fell to a very low priority. Their rationale for refusing the Lord's specific instructions was opposition by enemies, who would rather see them serve personal interests than obey Israel's God.

"Your fathers, where are they?" the prophet asked (1:5). The former prophets were are all dead, but their passing had not negated God's commands. In other words, Zechariah cried out to the people to get on with the Lord's work. If they refused, they would experience the same affliction visited upon their fathers.

Twenty-five hundred years later, we too live in a generation far more concerned about material comforts and prosperity than about the work of the Lord. But the message of God is timeless and its applications always current. We therefore will do well to take the message of this faithful Old Testament prophet to heart and seek to live in ways that honor the Lord. Our God and His desires must have the highest priority in our lives.

A Consideration of the Visions

Although the refugees who had returned from Babylon were building attractive homes and experiencing life in their homeland once again, Israel was still discouraged and distraught. They had reinstituted the sacrificial system after being home only six months (Ezra 3:6). An attempt to rebuild the Temple had been initiated by laying the foundation in the first month of the second year (Ezra 3:8-10). But enemies had disrupted their work (Ezra 4:1-5). This interruption in the construction brought on persistent frustration. In fact, they were unable to resume work on the Temple during the reign of Cyrus and into the reign of Darius (Ezra 4:5). Such was the situation when Zechariah began his prophecy (1:6).

Zechariah's message would lay to rest the idea that there was no hope for the beleaguered Jewish remnant. He would challenge them to renew the vision of rebuilding the Temple and fulfill the desire that had never really been out of their hearts. Indeed, he would reassure them that a sovereign God was still on His throne, and He was orchestrating a series of amazing events that would, in the end, bring it to pass.

When the adversaries of Judah and Benjamin heard that the Jews were rebuilding the Temple, they first sought to form an alliance with those tribes of Israel. They felt they could be convinced that it was bad policy to rebuild the national sanctuary. Zerubbabel and the other leaders courageously refused their offer. Not to be denied, these enemies became open in their opposition and hired counselors against them (Ezra 4:1-5). After some time, they gained a measure of success when King Artaxerxes, influenced by false accusations, commanded that work on the Temple be suspended (Ezra 4:23-24).

God responded to this conspiracy of evil by raising up two faithful men, Haggai and Zechariah, to bear His message. Then the Lord stirred up the Jewish elders, causing them to appeal directly to Darius the king regarding the matter of the *stop-work order* (Ezra 5:5). The king looked into the problem and discovered that the Jews had every right to rebuild their Temple because Cyrus, one of his predecessors, had so decreed many years before. Darius not only renewed the previous decree but was willing to do all he could to assist the Jews in the construction of their Temple, even to compelling the cooperation of their enemies (Ezra 6:8-12).

The conclusion of the situation is recorded in Ezra 6:14: "And the elders of the Jews built, and they prospered through the prophesying of Haggai, the prophet, and Zechariah, the son of Iddo. And they built and finished it, according to the commandment of the God of Israel, and according to the commandment of Cyrus, and Darius, and Artaxerxes, king of Persia."

Before all the related political matters were resolved and the *building permit* was reinstated, the Lord spoke to Zechariah through a series of visions, assuring the people that the Temple would be completed. In one very long, exhausting night, God gave Zechariah eight visions. They encompassed the rebuilding of the Temple and what would happen to the city of Jerusalem from that day until the end of time. These eight visions are recorded in the first six chapters of the book. We will examine each of them in detail and learn how God's plans unfolded for completing the Temple, guaranteeing the future of Jerusalem, and the long-term future of the nation of Israel.

Vision One: The Man Riding the Red Horse

First, we must note the timing of the visions. "Upon the four and twentieth day of the eleventh month, which is the month Shebat, in the second year of Darius, came the word of the LORD unto Zechariah, the son of Berechiah, the son of Iddo, the prophet" (1:7). Comparing verses 1 and 7 shows that these visions came on a night two to three months after Zechariah was given God's command to challenge the people to forsake the ways of their fathers and turn wholly to the Lord.

"I saw by night, and behold a man riding upon a red horse, and he stood among the myrtle trees that were in the bottom; and behind him were there red horses, sorrel, and white" (1:8). Although the rider is not identified at this point in the passage, there seems to be something unique about him. The words *behold a man* in the original Hebrew dramatically focus attention on the rider of the red horse; there is something very unusual about him. At the end of verse 8 horses of other colors are mentioned, but their riders are not, thus magnifying the prominence of this one rider. Is there something superhuman about this person? We shall have an answer to this question as we further explore the passage.

To determine what is unfolding, we need only compare this passage with Revelation 6, where four horsemen are pictured riding horses of colors similar to the horses in Zechariah, each representing something different. Revelation 6:4 describes a red horse and its rider: "And there went out another horse that was red; and power was given to him that sat on it to take peace from the earth, and that they should kill one another."

The red horse is a prophetic symbol of war. When this horse and rider enter the scene, peace will be removed from the earth and fighting will break out in diverse places. War will be the order of the day and will result in wholesale slaughter.

The passage in Revelation 6 amplifies the meaning of this first vision given to Zechariah. He had just encouraged the Jews to get on with the task of building the Temple. Then, by prophetic imagery, he showed Israel an angelic host standing by, led by the rider on the red horse. This man, along with his host, was watching over the nation of Israel and was ready to fight on behalf of the remnant of Jewish refugees who had returned to Jerusalem. That fact in itself was a tremendous source of encouragement for this Jewish remnant.

The Myrtle Trees

The rider of the red horse was standing among the myrtle trees. These trees, rarely more than eight to ten feet tall, are quite common in Israel. They flourish best in low-lying, well-watered areas and are often found along a riverbank. Myrtle trees have glossy leaves and produce star-shaped white flowers. When myrtle leaves are crushed, they emit a heavy, sweet fragrance.

The word in the Hebrew from which the word *myrtle* derives is fascinating. The name *Esther* comes from the same root. "And he brought up Hadassah, that is, Esther, his uncle's daughter" (Est. 2:7). We know that the Book of Esther deals with God's watch care over His dispersed people. Although they were crushed, as it were, they were still precious in God's sight. Downtrodden, defeated, and dispersed, they did and still do emit a sweet fragrance that is beautiful to God. The myrtle tree and Esther both provide a picture of a persecuted people who nevertheless give forth a rich fragrance, like someone who walks by, leaving behind a fragrance that lingers in the air for a while. Our lives should be the same to God as well as to those we meet—a fragrance that lingers, pleasing the Lord we love.

The myrtle trees were usually found in a low place, a bottom or glen. East, west, and south of the ancient city of Jerusalem are three valleys. To the east and running north and south is the Kidron Valley, and to the west running in the same direction is the Tyropoeon Valley. Both empty into the Valley of Hinnom, a portion of which is sometimes called Gehenna. The point at which the Valleys of Kidron and Hinnom meet was in ancient times called "the bottom." It was often referred to as "the hollow" or "the king's garden" (2 Ki. 25:4). The valley may represent the condition of Israel at that time, for they were certainly in a spiritual and emotional valley.

Let us review what we have learned thus far from the vision. The little body of discouraged Jews was living huddled in "the bottom" below Jerusalem. Daily they looked up at sacred Moriah and wondered what would come to pass. Their once-fervent desire to rebuild their Temple had been squelched. Work on the mount was still suspended, and disappointment was their daily companion. Through the Prophet Zechariah, the Lord gave them their first word of encouragement in 18 years. They were not alone in that valley. The rider on the red horse was guarding them and was ready to do battle on their behalf.

We who know the Lord should always remember that, just like Israel, believers have someone to lift them from discouragement and the uncertainties of the future. Jesus Christ said, "I will never leave thee, nor forsake thee" (Heb. 13:5). Believers have "a friend who sticketh closer than a brother" (Prov. 18:24).

Who Is the Rider on the Red Horse?

A clue to the rider's identity is given at the end of verse 8: "behind him were there red horses, sorrel, and white." Other horses followed this red horse that carried a rider. Without looking further, we sense that these horses also have riders and that those riders could be special beings.

Zechariah's pattern throughout the vision episodes was to question what he did not understand. Another personage, a communicating angel, appeared on the scene when the prophet needed an answer: "And the angel who talked with me said unto me, I will show thee what these are" (Zech. 1:9). The answer to his question regarding the identity of the rider on the red horse comes in verse 10: "These are they whom the LORD hath sent to walk to and fro through the earth." Obviously, the riders were angelic beings dispatched to search out the earth and report back to heaven on what was going on around the world. Their answer was, "behold, all the earth sitteth still, and is at rest" (v. 11). Peace prevailed around the world.

But who is this rider on the red horse? In verse 8 he is called "a man." In verse 11 he is called "the angel of the LORD." Finally, in verse 13 he is called "the LORD." The rider on the red horse was none other than God in the flesh. He was Israel's Messiah, the preincarnate Christ, ready to do battle for this Jewish remnant that had almost given up hope. God had not forgotten them, nor had He forsaken them. He was personally on the scene to accomplish His will and purposes for His beloved Israel. With this in view, it was no time for discouragement. Their victory was assured.

We will do well to pause at this point and apply this revelation to our situation today. If we focus our eyes on the world around us, we can become just as disillusioned as the Jewish people of Zechariah's day. But by living in the Word of God and focusing our eyes on the Lord, we obtain a very different perspective, for in spite of the desperate state of the situation surrounding us, God's promises and plans are being carried out before our very eyes. As children of God, we are part of that plan, and He is with us every step of the way.

The Lord's Promises for Jerusalem

The question posed in verse 12 was the same question that had been welling up in the hearts of the refugees: "O LORD of hosts, how long wilt thou not have mercy on Jerusalem and on the cities of Judah, against which thou hast had indignation these threescore and ten years?" The 70 years of captivity had ended, but when would the Lord show His mercy and allow the rebuilding to move forward? The answer is found in verse 16: "Therefore, thus saith the LORD: I am returned to Jerusalem with mercies; my house shall be built in it." They had their answer, given clearly and directly in this vision. Zechariah received the promise of the Lord for the people. He was already there, the city belonged to Him, and the rebuilding of the Temple was only a matter of time. The Lord had given them a promise, and He would fulfill it.

The Lord's Jealousy for Jerusalem

Zechariah was given "good words and comforting words" (v. 13) concerning the Jewish people and Jerusalem. He was instructed to "Cry" out this message, to shout it from the hilltops. "I am jealous for Jerusalem and for Zion with a great jealousy" (1:14b). This divine jealousy was closely related to the divine anger expressed in verse 2. The perfect tense used in the Hebrew conveys the sense that God had continually been jealous for His people, even though it was not evident to the people during the years of captivity and their dismal experiences after returning from Babylon. The word *jealousy* comes from the root of the verb in the intensive form that means to *burn* or *glow*. "Jealous . . . with a great jealousy" further emphasizes the concept (cp. Joel 2:18; Zech. 8:2). God's jealousy is very different from mankind's jealousy. It is a pure and holy desire to guard and keep for Himself those who belong to Him. God's feelings about Israel are often expressed in these terms in the Scriptures. He was never aloof from their needs but concerned and involved in every event in their lives. He is, of course, no less concerned about believers today.

Just as the Lord gave loving attention to every detail of the lives of those struggling Jews who had returned to Jerusalem, so too is He concerned about us. Nothing escapes His view. The greatest comfort available to us is recognizing that nothing can come into the life of a believer that God does not anticipate. His loving sovereignty reaches into the smallest details of our lives. We therefore can totally and confidently rest in Him. His care for the sparrow that falls illustrates His tender watch care over His own.

The Lord expressed His deep love for Israel in verse 14 but then showed His righteous anger in the following verse. "And I am very much displeased with the nations that are at ease; for I was but a little displeased, and they helped forward the affliction" (1:15). We can almost feel the heat of God's anger reflected in this verse. Just as verse 14 expressed God's love to the Jewish people, in verse 15 His fury, wrath, and fierce anger were turned upon the Gentile nations who, with God's permission, had conquered His people. Nonetheless, He would vent His wrath on those who had taken pleasure in afflicting Israel.

Why is this so? Although He had sent them to conquer His people because of their sin and idolatry, the nations that God had raised up to punish His people for those 70 years had gone too far. They had cruelly overstepped their bounds and become greater adversaries than God had intended them to be. They had gone so far as to try to annihilate His people, and now they faced God's wrath. This is the basis of Zechariah's second vision in verses 18 to 21.

The phrase "the nations that are at ease" seems almost out of place. Some have claimed that it means there was no war at the time the prophet wrote this book. Although that may be true, a far deeper meaning can be discovered by looking at other portions of Scripture where this same phrase is used.

In at least eight places where the Hebrew phrase translated "at ease" occurs, it is used in a derogatory way. "Because thy rage [ease] against me and thy tumult are come up into mine ears, therefore I will put my hook in thy nose" (2 Ki. 19:28a; cp. Isa. 37:29). It is a description of arrogance. God's anger, or "zeal," was aroused by this "ease" (2 Ki. 19:31). The word *ease* is also used in Psalm 123:4, where those "at ease" are the proud. In Amos 6:1 the phrase is used of those trusting "in the mountain of Samaria" rather than in the Lord.

Clearly the Lord was vehemently displeased with those nations who, by going beyond His bounds in chastening the Jewish people, displayed pride and arrogance and refused to trust in Him. Zechariah was the human instrument God used to trumpet the downfall of all nations who dare come against Israel. At the same time, he would sound the word of blessing in store for Jerusalem.

"Therefore, thus saith the LORD: I am returned to Jerusalem with mercies" (1:16). This was a great message of hope to that ragtag remnant of Jews living in the valley south of Jerusalem. Thwarted in their every effort to rebuild their Temple, they received their first words of encouragement. In essence, God said, In spite of what you may have thought, I'm in your midst. Your enemies will not prevail. I will deal with you in mercy.

Another basic thought arises from the Hebrew grammar of this verse. God's words are expressed in the prophetic perfect tense, speaking of a future event as if it had already occurred. That event is the coming of the Messiah to Jerusalem, and it was their assurance that their immediate desire would be fulfilled. Their Temple would be completed because God Himself would see to it that it was built. But the near-term building of the Temple was only a partial fulfillment of the promise. A far greater Temple was yet to be built, with a far greater high priest.

That part of the fulfillment awaits the day of the literal kingdom of God on the earth.

The promise that "a line shall be stretched forth upon Jerusalem" (1:16) refers to a day in Israel's future. God was preparing to intervene directly. In Zechariah 2:1 to 5 a young man with a measuring line in his hand is told not to measure the city because it will be so exceedingly large that it will not be measurable. In that day the glory of God will be in the city's midst, and He will be its protector. There will be no need of a physical military force. The measuring line of verse 16 linked with verse 17 indicates preparation for the days of prosperity that were to come to this remnant of returned Jews. God's blessings on Jerusalem would be seen in their lifetime, but even greater blessings lay ahead in the kingdom age.

A Jewish person reading these promises of future glory for the city might question the validity of the statements. Jerusalem has been a primary battleground for many of the world's armies for almost two millennia. In the process, Jewish people have been persecuted and dispersed. Even today, the world's focus is again on the unrest and conflict in Jerusalem. How then, one might well ask, can such statements about peace and prosperity be true?

The only rational answer is that God is in control! As the sovereign of history, in His time He will bring to a climax the events of world history. Jerusalem will be His city with the Messiah Jesus reigning as King. It is a biblically established fact that the beloved city is at the very heart of His plans for the millennial future. During the Millennial Kingdom, Jerusalem, the city of peace, will finally be at rest and will know the peace it has so long desired. And we can be personally assured that as Jerusalem will know peace when Christ returns to rule there, we, as individuals, can have peace with God now through faith in the one who will bring tranquility to Jerusalem. For individuals seeking peace with God, the most significant event in the history of Jerusalem occurred when the Messiah of Israel carried His cross outside the city walls nearly two thousand years ago. Then, as a jeering mob looked on, He was nailed to that tree, hung there, and died. His sacrificial act paid the awful price for our sins. In other words, He died in our place, as our substitute, that we might have peace with God. To obtain that peace, we must receive Him by faith as our Savior. Only then are we brought into a right relationship with God and are able to experience the joy of eternal peace.

Vision Two: The Four Horns and the Four Artisans

At the conclusion of the first vision, the Lord gave His assurance that He had returned to Jerusalem and that the Temple would be rebuilt. This was good news to the remnant of Jews gathered below the city, waiting for an answer from the Lord. The remnant could take comfort in the fact that the Lord had chosen Jerusalem as His own, and they would prosper in the place of their inheritance.

The Four Horns

> Then lifted I up mine eyes, and saw, and behold four horns. And I said unto the angel who talked with me, What are these? And he answered me, These are the horns which have scattered Judah, Israel, and Jerusalem (1:18-19).

Grateful but weary after receiving the first vision, Zechariah closed his eyes. Perhaps he was pondering in his heart the things he had been privileged to see. He may even have begun to fall asleep. But sleep was not an option, for God had much more to reveal to him about the future of His city and His people.

On five different occasions the prophet lifted up his eyes to receive a vision and a message from the communicating angel (1:18; 2:1; 5:1, 5; 6:1).

In the second vision, when Zechariah looked up he immediately saw four horns (1:18). Reacting to the strange sight, he asked the meaning of the message being communicated to him in the vision. "What are these?" he inquired (1:19). Perhaps because his grandfather Iddo was a prophet (1:1), he knew that a horn in a prophetic communication represented power or kingship (Dan. 7:24). Verse 21 reveals that each horn represented a Gentile world power.

Zechariah was told by the angel, "These are the horns which have scattered Judah, Israel, and Jerusalem" (1:19). He was given a parallel message to the one given to Daniel (cp. Dan. 2:36-44; 7:3-7). Four horns, or Gentile powers, would affect the course of history of his people, his nation, and the city of Jerusalem. By comparing parallel passages in other prophetic Scriptures, particularly Daniel, we know these nations or powers to be Babylon, the Medo-Persian Empire, Greece, and Rome. As each of these powers encountered Israel, they accomplished a specific element of prophetic truth.

The Four Artisans

And the LORD showed me four artisans. Then said I, What come
these to do? And he spoke, saying, These are the horns which have
scattered Judah, so that no man did lift up his head; but these are
come to terrify them, to cast out the horns of the nations, which lifted
up their horn over the land of Judah to scatter it (1:20-21).

The word translated *artisans* could probably have been better translated *smiths*. The term designates craftsmen who are trained and skilled
at working with their hands. Four such artisans came upon the scene
and became involved with the horns, or Gentile powers. The powers
were so effective, we are told, "that no man did lift up his head" (v.
21). No existing national power was strong enough to prevent their
conquering Judah, Israel, and Jerusalem and scattering the people.

The Relationship of the Horns to the Artisans

The introduction of the artisans presents a twist in the Scriptures that
is unique to the Book of Zechariah. Each horn became an artisan.

On several occasions in Scripture, the Lord allowed a person or a
nation to punish either a portion or all of the Jewish nation for their sin
and idolatry. They were God's chosen people, to be sure, but when
they turned away from Him, they were chastised for their disobedience.
Sadly, when the Lord allowed a nation or an individual leader to punish
His people, that punishment was often inflicted with vengeance exceed-
ing what was necessary to accomplish the divine purpose. In response
to such Gentile excesses, God intervened and punished those He had
used to correct His wayward people.

This truth explains the relationship between the horns and the
artisans. God would raise up a horn, or power, to punish rebellious
Israel. When that power overstepped its bounds, punishing God's
people beyond His intention, the Lord would intervene by raising up
another nation and leader (artisan) to subdue the failed power. The new
artisan, in turn, would rise to empire status and, in the process, gain
power, prestige, and wealth. The new empire usually lasted for several
hundred years before being replaced by a new horn. Each new horn
was used to carry out a phase of disciplining Israel when the nation
began to slip into apostasy. In due time, each new horn, in its turn,
overstepped God's limitations, and, in response, the Lord raised up

another artisan nation. The cycle was reenacted throughout the history
of the four major empires named in the Scriptures (Babylonian Empire,
586 to 450 B.C.; Medo-Persian Empire, 450 to 330 B.C.; Greek Empire,
330 to 166 B.C.; and Roman Empire, 63 B.C. to 330 A.D.).
The Babylonian Empire, identified as the first horn, was the first
Gentile world power unveiled in the dream of Nebuchadnezzar (Dan.
2) and the subsequent dream and vision of Daniel (Dan. 7). The first
artisan was the Medo-Persian Empire. The Medes and Persians suc-
ceeded Babylon to become the next horn. Eventually they too became
oppressors of God's people and fell victim to the next artisan, the
Grecian Empire. Finally, Rome, the last great empire, came on the
scene as the artisan that destroyed the Grecian Empire.

It is noteworthy that the fourth artisan is missing. No nation has come
upon the world scene to decisively depose Rome. And we would do
well to remember that the Roman Empire so crushed the Jewish people
that they were sent into dispersion for nearly two thousand years.
Although Rome was, in time, fragmented by internal corruption, the
empire was never really destroyed. It is of no little significance that the
spirit of Rome is still in existence, and, as the Scriptures emphatically
point out, a major portion of that empire will be reassembled in the end
times.

An intriguing question then begs to be answered: Who is the fourth
and final artisan? Daniel refers to Him as a "stone . . . cut
out . . . without hands" (Dan. 2:45) that will fall on all the Gentile
nations, destroy them, and become the ruler of a kingdom that "the
God of heaven set up . . . which shall never be destroyed" (Dan. 2:44).
These words make it exceedingly clear that the stone is Jesus Christ,
and the kingdom identified will be established and ruled over by the
triumphant Messiah. This historical certainty causes every humanly
crafted empire to pale into insignificance. As a matter of fact, all such
earthly authorities will be subdued as the King takes His throne.

Appropriately, Jesus will rule over the earth from Jerusalem amid
reconciled Israel, the very nation that other horn kingdoms have sought
to destroy. Unfortunately, empirical obsession to destroy Israel has
outlived ancient perpetrators, for even today movements around the
world are attempting to accomplish the satanic objective. For example,
Pamyat, a hate group in Russia, has set the destruction of Judaism as a
fundamental goal of the movement (see *Newsweek*, May 7, 1990).
Neo-Nazis, who are growing in numbers throughout the Western world,

share this passion to destroy the Jews. Scriptures have forewarned that such activities will only worsen as the world moves deeper into the end times and will expand explosively as the Antichrist vents Satan's wrath on the Jewish people during the Tribulation period.

Zechariah's vision indeed reveals that this fourth artisan will surely come to do His work in harmony with the perfect will of God. Jesus will, once and for all, rid the world of anti-Semitism and establish God's kingdom rule in the land of Israel, the city of Jerusalem, and among the people of God who have been so long troubled by Gentile oppressors.

This assurance can cause believers of every century to take heart, for no matter how terrible the world situation becomes, we live in the confidence that God is still on the throne. He will prevail. Christ will win the battle, and we who are in Christ are on the victory side.

What a blessing Zechariah's prophecy was for the discouraged band of Jews in the valley just below Jerusalem. Even if nothing more had been written, they would have learned four important things: Their Temple would soon be rebuilt; prosperity would return to their land; God would comfort Zion and choose Jerusalem for His own; and God would eventually recompense the Gentile nations.

ENDNOTES

[1]Feinberg, Dr. Charles, *God Remembers, A Study of Zechariah* (Portland, Oregon: Multnomah Press, 1965), p. 45.

ZECHARIAH 2

Vision Three: The Divine Protector of Jerusalem

For the second time in as many chapters, the Word records that Zechariah lifted up his eyes. This may signify weariness or perhaps a state of deep contemplation over the first two visions. Incidentally, all eight visions recorded in chapters 1 through 6 came to Zechariah in one night. Thus, it is understandable that the prophet may have been overwhelmed by the sheer volume of the revelations.

In the two visions examined thus far, we have learned that the rider on the red horse provided a picture of hope for a downtrodden Israel and that the horns and artisans portrayed the fact that the nations trampling Jerusalem would be crushed by an avenging God. In this third vision the Lord revealed that the hope of Jerusalem will be realized when the conquering nations are crushed and Jerusalem is exalted. The future glory of the city of peace will far surpass the scope of human imagination.

The Persons in the Vision

"Behold a man with a measuring line in his hand" (2:1). Our attention is drawn to this man, who is highlighted by the verb *behold* or *look*. He has obviously been commissioned to measure something of great significance to God.

"Then said I, Where goest thou? And he said unto me, To measure Jerusalem, to see what is the breadth of it, and what is its length" (2:2).

Who was this man sent to survey the boundaries of the city?

Among the persons involved with the vision is the angel who communicated with Zechariah. In verse 3 another angel went out to meet the man with the measuring line, and verse 4 speaks of someone called "young man." This young man was apparently Zechariah himself. He was the one who originally posed the question to the man carrying the line. There is reason to believe that the man with the measuring line in his hand was the "angel of the LORD," perhaps the preincarnate Christ.

The terminology used here is consistent with other passages referring to the Messiah. For example, the same phrase, "behold a man," appears in Zechariah 1:8. In this instance, it refers to the man riding on a red horse, later identified as the "angel of the LORD" (1:11-12) and also as "the LORD" or Jehovah (1:13). Zechariah 6:12 refers to one called "THE BRANCH": "Behold, the man whose name is THE BRANCH." "BRANCH" has strong messianic connotations.

Finally, the Prophet Ezekiel said, "behold, there was a man, whose appearance was like the appearance of bronze, with a line of flax in his hand, and a measuring reed; and he stood in the gate" (Ezek. 40:3). This is obviously a messianic prophecy and refers to the one going out to measure the future Temple in the city of Jerusalem as Israel's long-awaited one, the Messiah.

A City Without Walls for Protection

Three basic promises were given to the prophet in this very brief segment. The first was, "Jerusalem shall be inhabited like towns without walls for the multitude of men and cattle in it" (2:4b). This first promise describes something unheard of in the ancient world.

When an ancient city was built, two elements were considered necessary. First, it was essential to secure an adequate water supply. Jerusalem is a good example of a city that has this resource. Second, the city must be defensible. The most desirable location on which to build, if available, was the summit of a hill. To augment this advantage, massive walls often surrounded the city.

Jerusalem was a walled city long before the Prophet Zechariah came on the scene. Although its walls shifted somewhat as the population grew, the old city of Zion was known for its walls. As history demonstrates, the walls of Jerusalem were severely tested in ancient and modern times.

But in a statement that, at first glance, appears rather incomprehensible, the prophet was told by Jehovah that in the future Jerusalem will not have walls. Such a multitude of people and animals will inhabit the city that it will be impossible to maintain the traditional defense system. We can imagine the prophet's perplexity when he heard this pronouncement. In his day, only a relative handful of Jewish people had returned from the Babylonian captivity and were living in Jerusalem. A major endeavor for the remnant was to rebuild the walls broken down by the conquering Babylonians. Zechariah could scarcely imagine a city so densely populated that walls could not contain the people or be deemed necessary.

Exciting news required the angelic messenger to move with haste. "Run" he was told (2:4). Communicating the prediction that Jerusalem's population would far exceed any previous boundaries carried a sense of urgency.

In Isaiah 49:19 to 20 we read that this expansion of Jerusalem will come in a future day: "For thy waste and thy desolate places, and the land of thy destruction, shall even now be too narrow by reason of the inhabitants, and they that swallowed thee up shall be far away. The children whom thou shalt have, after thou hast lost the other, shall say again in thine ears, The place is too narrow for me; give a place to me that I may dwell."

Furthermore, the Prophet Ezekiel spoke of a measured Temple area at that time that will be far larger than we can imagine. One Jewish source says, "In the future the gates of Jerusalem will reach to Damascus" (Sifre Debarim 1).[1]

Today Jerusalem is expanding rapidly to the north and west. Such expansion serves as a reminder of the growth to be consummated in the Millennium.

A City With a Wall of Fire

The second promise was, "I, saith the LORD, will be unto it a wall of fire round about" (2:5a). No man-made walls will be needed when the Lord Himself becomes the protector of the city.

For primitive man, fire served to keep marauding animals away, especially at night. During Israel's wilderness sojourn, the Lord put in the midst of the camp a covering of cloud by day and a pillar of fire by night. The cloud and fire signified that God was in the midst of His people. Israel's Shekinah light embodied the very glory of the Lord; thus, He demonstrated His presence throughout their wilderness wanderings. In this passage, however, He offered even more. A protecting wall of fire would surround Jerusalem and provide security for the inhabitants.

A City Full of God's Glory

Although the glory of God in the cloud and pillar of fire once dwelt in the midst of ancient Israel, idolatry caused His glory to leave the Temple. In a dramatic portrayal of the departure of God's glory from the Temple, the Shekinah passed through the Eastern Gate and left Jerusalem and Israel via the Mount of Olives. The solemn epitaph, *Ichabod (the glory is departed)* [1 Sam. 4:21], was, from that day, written over the city.

The process of God's glory leaving the Temple and then the city of Jerusalem is recorded in the prophecy of Ezekiel. "And, behold, the glory of the God of Israel was there, according to the vision that I saw in the plain" (Ezek. 8:4). Divine long-suffering during prolonged periods of wickedness and idolatry kept the glory of God in the Temple in Jerusalem. But one day the cup of God's indignation over their sins was full, and the glory was withdrawn.

Ezekiel was taken inside the Temple of Solomon, which had been dedicated to the Lord nearly 400 years before. At that dedication the glory of the Lord had descended, entered the holy of holies, and remained there over the intervening years. But as he went into the heart of the Temple, Ezekiel discovered one abomination after another (Ezek. 8:5-18). He saw the elders of Israel bowing to heathen idols within the confines of God's dwelling place. Worship of false gods was common, including Tammuz, the Babylonian goddess of fertility, and the sun god. Israel had once again reached the limits of God's endurance.

We can follow the sad progression as the glory of God departed from the Temple. "And the glory of the God of Israel was gone up from the cherub, upon which he was, to the threshold of the house" (Ezek. 9:3). This was the first step. God's glory left its resting place over the cherubim. "Then the glory of the LORD departed from off the threshold of the house, and stood over the cherubim" (Ezek. 10:18). This was the next step. "Then did the cherubim lift up their wings, and the wheels beside them; and the glory of the God of Israel was over them above. And the glory of the LORD went up from the midst of the city, and stood upon the mountain which is on the east side of the city" (Ezek. 11:22-23). By way of the Mount of Olives, the glory of God left Israel approximately seven years before Nebuchadnezzar and the Chaldean troops entered Jerusalem. They destroyed the city, burned the Temple, killed a multitude of Jews, and carried most of the remaining residents into captivity in Babylon. Once the glory of God departed, the city no longer had a divine protector and so inevitably fell to its enemy.

We cannot begin to imagine what it meant to Zechariah for the Lord to say to him, "I . . . will be the glory in the midst of it" (2:5b). He knew that protection and safety would accompany the return of the glory of God. Adding this promise to that of the first vision in Zechariah 1:16, "Therefore, thus saith the LORD: I am returned to Jerusalem with mercies," shows how God lifted that discouraged band of released captives from tears and despondency to relief and hope in their immediate situation.

Zechariah 2:4 to 5 also contains a long-range prediction for the Jewish people; in fact, it uses words identical to those of Ezekiel. It promised that the Lord would dwell among them and protect them during the kingdom age. But, as was so often true with the people of the period, they soon drifted away from the Lord again, this time into Pharisaism and legalism. The latter prophets fared no better in calling the people to national repentance. As a result, God silenced His prophets, and for 400 years no voice of the prophet was heard in the land.

But God had not utterly forsaken the people so close to His heart. And one night, as shepherds watched their flocks, "an angel of the Lord came upon them, and the glory of the Lord shone round about them; and they were very much afraid" (Lk. 2:9). The glory of God had returned to the earth, and at the center of that greatest of all lights was the person of Jesus Christ. "Glory to God in the highest," the angelic host shouted (Lk. 2:14). Once again God's glory had come to the earth to live among mankind. "And we beheld his glory, the glory as of the only begotten of the Father" (Jn. 1:14).

In Christ, the glory of God was incarnate. But although He walked the earth, rebellion by God's own was once again present (Jn. 1:11). His rejection by the nation's leadership eventually led to the Messiah's crucifixion and resurrection. Of immense interest is the fact that following His resurrection, when He ascended to heaven, Jesus traveled the same route as the glory of God had in Ezekiel's account of the Shekinah's departure. He left the city through the Eastern Gate and moved on to the Mount of Olives, from which He ascended. With His departure, the glory of God was gone once again. But secreted in Zechariah's third vision, with its promise of a greatly enlarged Jerusalem in the future, is an account of the return of the glory of God to the earth when His Son returns in glory to rule and reign as King of kings:

"For I, saith the LORD, will be . . . the glory in the midst of it" (2:5b).
"And he shall bear the glory, and shall sit and rule upon his throne"
(Zech. 6:13).

Surveying this vision might prompt one to ask just what all this has
to do with us today. Actually, it has much to do with those of us who
know the Lord. Although no literal, physical temple of God exists on
the earth today, the children of God are the temple of the Holy Spirit.
In other words, the actual glory of God dwells in those who are
believers. Thus, as we look into the face of our Lord through His Word
and walk in fellowship and communion with Him, we become reflectors
of His glory. Therefore, the way we live daily constantly radiates His
glory to a lost world.

Paul explained in 2 Corinthians: "But we all, with unveiled face
beholding as in a mirror the glory of the Lord, are changed into the
same image from glory to glory, even as by the Spirit of the Lord"
(2 Cor. 3:18); "For God, who commanded the light to shine out of
darkness, hath shone in our hearts, to give the light of the knowledge
of the glory of God in the face of Jesus Christ. But we have this treasure
in earthen vessels, that the excellency of the power may be of God, and
not of us" (2 Cor. 4:6-7).

The Prophetic Address of Zechariah

After the consolation given to Israel in the third vision, Zechariah
issued a stern warning to the Jewish people still living in Babylon.
Actually, they were the great majority of the Jewish population, for
only a small number had returned to Jerusalem.

When we first read "Ho, ho" in verse 6, we may be tempted to think
of laughter. But that is certainly not the idea here. Rather, it is the same
phrase used in Isaiah 55:1, "Ho, every one that thirsteth." It is used
to get people's attention. A good paraphrase would be, Listen to this;
something important is coming. And it was indeed.

The Protection in Jerusalem

As stated previously, only a handful of the Jewish exiles of the
Babylonian captivity had returned to their homeland. The majority had
stayed behind, and their lives had become deeply rooted in Babylon
and other places where they had lived for decades. Some, like Jeremiah,

went to Egypt (Jer. 43:7), while others went to Moab, Ammon, and Edom (Jer. 40:11-12). And so, rather than being restricted to one region, the Jews were scattered throughout the Middle East. In the nearly 70 years that they lived outside their homeland, another generation had been born, grown, and settled down. Business was good, and life was comfortable. Consequently, many were not interested in returning home.

Zechariah called for them to leave their present comfort and return to Jerusalem. His startling declaration came from the Lord in the form of a command: "come forth, and flee from the land of the north, saith the LORD; for I have spread you abroad as the four winds of the heavens, saith the LORD. Deliver thyself, O Zion, that dwellest with the daughter of Babylon" (2:6-7).

Great changes were coming. Little did the scattered exiles know that within a few years the proud, pompous Chaldean kingdom would suddenly fall. God used Zechariah to warn the exiles who remained outside of Israel to return home. If they remained in those foreign places, their lives would be in jeopardy. If they returned to the land, they would again be under the blessing and protection of God.

The armies of Darius the Mede would soon and swiftly take Babylon, and those armies would not distinguish between nationalities. Jewish exiles would die alongside Chaldeans. The message to flee Babylon was not unique to Zechariah. More than 150 years earlier Isaiah said, "Go forth from Babylon, flee from the Chaldeans; with a voice of singing declare, tell this, utter it even to the end of the earth; say: The LORD hath redeemed his servant Jacob" (Isa. 48:20). Jeremiah gave a similar cry: "Flee out of the midst of Babylon, and deliver every man his soul" (Jer. 51:6).

A Spiritual Lesson for Today

Babylon throughout Scripture is a picture of the world. Beginning in Genesis and continuing through Revelation 17 and 18, it is also a picture of the world's evil system. Just as God commanded the Jews to flee from that physical land, He commands and pleads with His children today not to get caught up in the system of this world. We are to be separated wholly unto Him, fleeing the predominantly evil system of our time. Just as the Lord urged the Jews to return home, He strongly urges us to return home spiritually by separating ourselves from the world system.

Verse 6 says, "flee from the land of the north," referring to the entire region north of Israel that was known as Mesopotamia. Verse 7 states, "Deliver thyself, O Zion, that dwellest with the daughter of Babylon." God expressed His will in a marvelous way. The children of Israel had been scattered by God, but He pleaded with them to return home of their own free will. He would not force them to return, but He urged them very strongly to do so.

God was planning to judge Babylon. Although she had been commissioned by the Lord to take Israel captive, she had overstepped the bounds of the Lord's intention for her with regard to Israel. As a result, He intended that she would suffer great humiliation and defeat. There would soon come a major world power shift from Babylon to Media and then Persia. As always, the Lord was carefully watching over His people. He clearly warned them to run home to His protection. Through His compassionate call for Israel to flee Babylon, we can readily see the lesson for us today.

The Punishment of the Nations

The first half of verse 8 is probably the most difficult portion of the entire book both to translate and to interpret. The prophet had just conveyed God's command to the Jewish people to flee from Babylon and the other nations where they had taken refuge. He went on to tell the reason for the command.

The problem is with the phrase, "After the glory." What does it mean, and of whom is it speaking? Some believe that because there is no definite article *the* in the phrase, it refers to a time after the glorious Second Coming of the Lord. The problem with this interpretation is that we know the Lord will not go out and "shake [His] hand" (2:9) on the nations after His kingdom is established and He is dwelling among His people. This appears to be a picture of the Messiah coming to vindicate Himself and visit judgment on all the nations that have raped, pillaged, and plundered Israel. That judgment will not be limited to Babylon. The passage presents a perspective far broader than that of judgment against one nation.

Verse 8 declares that the Messiah is sent to "the nations which spoiled you." It is also made very clear that "I [God] will shake mine hand upon them, and they shall be a spoil to their servants'' (2:9). This latter prophecy is an emphatic statement. By a gesture of His hand, the Lord will overthrow the nations. This is similar to Daniel's prophecy of a stone cut without hands that comes rolling down the mountain, smiting all the Gentile world powers. This will all be done by the hand of the Lord and not by mankind.

This portion of Scripture takes a herculean jump in time, prophetically speaking, from the fall of Babylon to a future day when the Lord will deal with all the nations that have touched Israel. It was exactly what He would do in just a few years to Israel's immediate persecutor, Babylon.

The phrase found toward the end of verse 8, "for he that toucheth you toucheth the apple of his eye," is not unique to Zechariah. It is used in several other places in the Old Testament. For example, Solomon used it in Proverbs 7:2 as he spoke to his sons. A son is to keep the "law as the apple of thine eye." The Word of God should be as dear to a young man as the apple or pupil of his own eye. The pupil is easily injured, often causing blindness, and it cannot be replaced.

In Psalm 17:8 David prayed to the Lord, "Keep me as the apple of the eye; hide me under the shadow of thy wings." He was casting himself upon the Lord. Apparently this psalm was written when David was being pursued by one of his many enemies, possibly King Saul.

Moses used this phrase in an intriguing way. "For the LORD's portion is his people; Jacob is the lot of his inheritance. He found him in a desert land, and in the waste, howling wilderness; he led him about, he instructed him, he kept him as the apple of his eye" (Dt. 32:9-10). The phrase is used in a protective sense over God's people Israel, who are dear to Him.

In verse 8 the phrase is used in relationship to what the Lord will do to the nations that have pillaged His people. Israel is truly a people over whom the Lord exercises very special care. Those who touch Israel will receive divine judgment and punishment.

Embedded in this portion is an important principle that we must learn: No matter what their situation, the Lord has placed Israel in a special position. The individual or nation that turns against Israel will have the blessing of God removed and will face His judgment. This should remind us of how the Lord views anti-Semitism.

The Promise of His Coming

To the discouraged exiles from Babylon, it seemed impossible to accomplish their purposed rebuilding of the Temple. In spite of this, two imperatives were placed before Israel by the Lord. They were to sing and rejoice. The phrase "daughter of Zion" (2:10) is used specifically for Jerusalem but also applies to the people in the surrounding area. This is clarified by verse 11, which refers to "many nations." Why should there be singing and rejoicing? Because, as is affirmed throughout the first two chapters of Zechariah's prophecy, the Lord will return. "I come," is the comforting word, "and I will dwell in the midst of thee . . . and thou shalt know that the LORD of hosts hath sent me unto thee" (2:10-11). The word for *dwell* is that from which the word *Shekinah* comes, indicating once again that God will permanently dwell with mankind.

This reference is to a great day when many nations will turn to the Lord. It is a prophecy far removed from the lifetime of Zechariah, a day that will see the nations turn to the Lord. These verses are unmistakably related to the Millennium, when Christ will dwell here on earth and fulfill the promise to return to Jerusalem.

The phrase "holy land" (2:12) needs a word of explanation. Currently, many naive pilgrims visit Israel expecting to find a "holy land." They learn, however, that it is far from holy. Less than 25 percent of the people are "religious." Israel is a secular, humanistic country. Like any other secular nation, most of the people are involved in work, play, and the exercise of their own wills. It is not spiritually a "holy land," although the country contains many religious shrines and "sacred" places.

Interestingly, this is the only place in the Scripture where Israel is called "the holy land." The statement alludes to its becoming a truly holy land when the Lord is there and the inhabitants, en masse, have turned to Him (Zech. 12:10).

The chapter reaches its climax in the last verse. "Be silent, O all flesh, before the LORD; for he is raised up out of his holy habitation" (2:13). In the presence of what has been revealed, mankind must stand in speechless awe. God is exercising His sovereign will. A similar concept is portrayed in Isaiah 52:15: "the kings shall shut their mouths at him." When the Lord, pictured in this text as being aroused out of His holy habitation, steps across time and space and intervenes in the end times, the world is told to be silent. In reality, they will have nothing to say. He will take absolute and complete control.

ENDNOTES

[1]Peter J. Colón, "Zechariah: A Historical and Prophetic Bible Study on Israel and Jerusalem" (unpublished).

ZECHARIAH 3

Vision Four: The Forgiveness of Israel's Sin

Israel's Hope Restored

The first three visions of Zechariah involve external blessings to the land and the people. God apparently gave the faithful prophet an overview of the history of the city of Jerusalem and informed him of a day when the Jewish people would be fully restored to their land. He also promised that the enemies of Israel would ultimately be destroyed, and their precious city would eventually be rebuilt and filled with a glory that would dim any past glory Jerusalem had ever known. Finally, the Lord proclaimed that He would be the protector of Jerusalem, for He would dwell within the city, making it His home.

To that struggling remnant who had returned from Babylon, this must have been a magnificent word of encouragement. They could get on with the business of rebuilding their Temple and city. God had not forgotten them.

Israel's High Priest Condemned

In chapter 3 the scene shifts from an overview of the city of Jerusalem, and the vision turns to the spiritual. The Word focuses on the Temple Mount, the Temple, and Joshua, its high priest.

To this point, nothing had been said or done about Israel's sins. This vision would alter the direction of Zechariah's revelation, for at this point the Holy Spirit began to deal with Israel's sins, which were so heinous to God.

Throughout the Hebrew Scriptures it is made clear that Israel will one day be judged for her sins. Although she had suffered terribly through the 70 years of Babylonian captivity, no evidence is given that she had repented or received God's pardon for her sins. She did learn a lesson about idolatry, but national repentance and forgiveness by God had not yet occurred.

The question addressed in this passage is simple and straightforward: How can a holy and righteous God restore such a sinful people to fellowship with Himself and still be consistent with His own holy character? The answer is found in the fourth vision given to Zechariah. It reveals precisely how Israel will be cleansed from her sins.

The Attack of Satan on the High Priest

In verses 1 to 3 Zechariah saw Joshua, the high priest, carrying on the function of intercession before the angel of the Lord: "And he showed me Joshua, the high priest, standing before the angel of the LORD, and Satan standing at his right hand to resist him" (3:1). Satan, the great adversary and opposer of God and His people, stood at the right hand of the angel of the Lord to oppose him. This is nothing new; it is what Satan has been doing since his fall. On this occasion he accused Joshua of standing before God in "filthy garments" (3:3). Incidentally, the Hebrew word translated *filthy* is *eban*, a much stronger word than its English translation. It means *dirty, foul-odored, and excrement-covered*. It was a lamentable view of the high priest of Israel standing accused and condemned before the Lord by Satan—indeed, a tragic condition.

As far as we can ascertain, Joshua was an actual historical figure who served as high priest of Israel. Apparently he had returned from Babylon with Zerubbabel. Joshua rebuilt the altar of God (Ezra 3:2) and was involved with laying the foundations of the Temple following the captivity (Ezra 3:8-10). He also refused the offers of the Samaritan adversaries to assist the Jews in building the Temple.

The Representation of the High Priest

The high priest of Israel was the nation's primary representative before God. He alone could enter into the presence of the Lord. Even then, he was allowed to go into the holy of holies only once a year, on the day of atonement, Yom Kippur. Then he could enter only after the blood of sacrificial animals was shed, first to cover his own sins and then to cover those of his people. The Jewish people themselves had no direct, personal access to God.

Under the Old Testament economy, the people received no forgiveness of sin, only covering of their sins. The New Testament Book of Hebrews offers an explanation and emphasizes the necessity of the final sacrifice through Christ. "For it is not possible that the blood of bulls and of goats should take away sins . . . And every priest standeth daily ministering and offering often the same sacrifices, which can never take away sins; But this man, after he had offered one sacrifice for sins forever, sat down on the right hand of God, From henceforth expecting till his enemies be made his footstool. For by one offering he hath perfected forever them that are sanctified" (Heb. 10:4, 11-14).

The important thing to note in Zechariah 3 is not who Joshua was as an individual but the position he held as high priest. He stood as the designated representative of the whole household of Israel. This is the emphasis around which the drama of the vision unfolded.

The Action of the Lord on Behalf of the High Priest

As Israel's high priest stood silent before the Lord, God intervened on behalf of both Joshua and the people of Israel. His voice rang out: "The LORD [Jehovah] rebuke thee, O Satan; even the LORD, who hath chosen Jerusalem, rebuke thee. Is not this a brand plucked out of the fire?" (3:2).

Israel had a defender—Jehovah Himself. Satan was severely rebuked and reminded that God Himself had chosen Israel and Jerusalem. In Deuteronomy 7:7 to 8 God had expressed His sovereign choice of His people, not because of who or what they were, but because of His will. His love for them was, regardless of the present situation, everlasting (Jer. 31:3). Dr. Charles Feinberg quotes one author as saying, "He chose you because He loved you; and He loved you because He loved you."[1]

Israel is pictured as "a brand plucked out of the fire." The reference is probably taken from Amos 4, where Israel was reminded of her transgressions by the Prophet Amos some 250 years earlier. Pleading with His people to return to Him, God said, "I have overthrown some of you, as God overthrew Sodom and Gomorrah, and ye were like a firebrand plucked out of the burning; yet have ye not returned unto me, saith the LORD" (Amos 4:11).

The image drawn is of Israel having been delivered from God's punishment while suffering in the Babylonian captivity. If He had not providentially delivered her, as a brand plucked from the fire, she would have been destroyed. God let Satan and the world know that Israel has a future. Her preservation assured better things to come.

We, too, should take heed of that judgment of burning fire from which the Lord has plucked us. Just as with Israel, although severe testing may come, His ultimate purpose is not to destroy us but to bless us forever.

Israel's Sin Removed

In verse 4 the angel of the Lord, the preincarnate Christ, spoke to other unnamed angelic beings: "Take away the filthy garments from him. And unto him he said, Behold, I have caused thine iniquity to pass from thee, and I will clothe thee with change of raiment."

First, the angel of the Lord told the other angelic beings standing by Joshua to remove the filthy robes from the high priest. Those robes represented the sin and uncleanness of the nation of Israel. We can be certain of this, for the passage says, "Behold, I have caused thine iniquity to pass from thee" (3:4). It points to a future day when, the writer says, God "will remove the iniquity of that land in one day" (3:9).

Second, neither Joshua nor Israel could do anything to remove their own iniquity. There is a wonderful present-day application here. None of us can do anything to rid ourselves of sin. Removal of our sins requires a pardon that can be given only through the grace of God. Whether the sins are Israel's or ours, sin can be forgiven only by divine intervention, which is what Calvary is all about. Jesus stepped across time and space to intervene in this world on behalf of lost Jews and Gentiles alike. By so doing, He paid the price for sin, thereby making it possible for mankind to be forgiven. In this way, the righteousness and holiness of God can be satisfied.

Third, the Lord said He would clothe the high priest with a change of raiment. Whereas the act of removing the filthy clothing speaks of justification, the new and festive clothes given to the high priest show that he and all believers can be made pure and clean before the Lord.

Zechariah's Request

The prophet became a participant in the vision at this point. He requested that those who were clothing Joshua "set a clean turban upon his head'' (3:5). In all probability this refers to the headdress the high priest wore (Ex. 28:36-38). Placed on this turban was a plate of pure gold engraved with the words, "HOLINESS TO THE LORD." Zechariah asked that the attire of the high priest be completed in order for Joshua to be totally equipped to carry out his duties.

Through this cleansing of Joshua the high priest, the Lord allows us to see a future cleansing of Israel. Although the Lord had previously promised physical deliverance to Israel in Zechariah 1 and 2, in this passage He allows us to glimpse that coming day of spiritual cleansing of the nation. Later in the book, God described a future high priest for Israel who will far surpass Joshua and every other high priest that the nation has ever known. He will be their Messiah, and once the nation is cleansed, the people will have permanent, direct, perfect access to God.

Joshua the High Priest Commissioned

A cleansed high priest needed a renewed commission, and Joshua received this in verses 6 and 7. The angel of the Lord "protested unto Joshua." The word *protested* is better translated *declared, charged*, or *admonished*. It means to *call God to witness*. It is the same Hebrew word used by Solomon to Shimei in 1 Kings 2:42: "Did I not make thee to swear by the LORD, and admonished thee . . . ?" The use of the word *protested* is therefore meant to express the importance of the declaration. Joshua was to "walk in [God's] ways" (3:7). This refers to his personal life. He was to pay strict attention to God's standards for his life. He was to make a total commitment to the Lord, setting aside anything that would turn him away from that commitment.

Joshua was also told to "keep [God's] charge" (3:7). He was to be faithful in his official duties to the Lord as well as in his personal life. This involved resolutely keeping the rituals laid down for priests. The same word is used nine times in Numbers 3. In essence, Joshua was to fulfill both the moral and ritual requirements of the Lord. As was true with this servant of God, anyone who is to serve the Lord properly must be totally committed to Him. Too often people try to serve the Lord without such a commitment and fail to bring glory to Him through their labors. Before we can truly serve the Lord, our lives must be holy. New believers are, at times, rushed into service before their walk with the Lord is stabilized or they have developed a degree of spiritual maturity. When this is the case, failure is virtually assured.

Verse 7 contains three promises to the recommissioned and cleansed high priest. First, God told Joshua that if he was obedient to the earlier commands in verse 7, "thou shalt . . . judge my house." The "house" could very well refer to the Temple, but the statement seems to have a broader meaning. "My house" may be used metaphorically of the people: "My servant, Moses, . . . is faithful in all mine house" (Num. 12:7); "Moses was faithful in all his house" (Heb. 3:2). Because Joshua was the representative of all of Israel before God, the meaning is likely that one of the rewards of a faithful life and true service was the God-given privilege of judging the whole house of Israel in matters of controversy, just as God granted Moses the same privilege and responsibility.

The second promise—to "keep [God's] courts" (3:7)—is probably far more limited. It seems that Joshua was granted the administration of the Temple that Zerubbabel was soon to complete. His responsibilities would be to watch over it and keep out anything of a defiling nature.

The third and final promise is most intriguing. "I will give thee places to walk among these who stand by" (3:7c). Those who stood by were angelic beings (see 3:4) who removed the filthy robes from Joshua. They stood in the presence of the Lord and did His bidding. It is certain that the promise to cleanse Joshua did not mean that he would become an angel because angels are an order of created beings distinct from humans. Two possible interpretations have been debated by theologians. Depending on the interpretation, this promise is seen to apply to either the present or eternity.

The ancient Jewish Targum paraphrases this portion to read, "In the resurrection of the dead I will receive thee, and give thee feet walking among these seraphim." Some believe, then, that in heaven Joshua will walk among the angelic beings.

Probably a more acceptable position is that Joshua would be rewarded for faithful service by walking among the angels in the Temple, with the reward of direct access to God. Joshua could commune with the God he served much like Moses did many years before. All Old Testament saints could pray, but a cleansed Joshua could be assured that the Lord would hear him.

The entire third chapter of Zechariah is a marvelous picture of the gospel of the Lord Jesus Christ. It gives a clear lesson on Isaiah 64:6, "But we are all as an unclean thing, and all our righteousnesses are as filthy rags; and we all do fade as a leaf, and our iniquities, like the wind, have taken us away." The angel of the Lord (Jesus Christ) comes in to take away our sins (those filthy rags) and give us a robe of righteousness (2 Cor. 5:21). We are transformed and plucked as a brand from the burning. Thus, believers become priests of God, with the promise of dwelling eternally with Him.

Therefore, New Testament believers have greater privileges than did Joshua. "For we have not an high priest who cannot be touched with the feeling of our infirmities, but was in all points tempted like as we are, yet without sin. Let us, therefore, come boldly unto the throne of grace, that we may obtain mercy, and find grace to help in time of need" (Heb. 4:15-16). We have direct access to the throne of God, but to have a close walk with the Lord we must have purity of heart, just as the Lord required of Joshua the high priest. Sin hinders prayer (Isa. 59:1-2). We must keep our minds and bodies pure to experience the blessing God has for us as we approach Him.

The Promise of a Greater High Priest

Following Joshua's cleansing and commission, the focus is centered on the High Priest who was yet to come. Beginning with verse 8, we take, as it were, a quantum leap through the centuries—from the high priest of Zechariah's day to the era of the eternal High Priest, Israel's Messiah, Jesus.

The words "Hear now" (3:8) call Israel's high priest to attention. Joshua and his fellows were to listen to an important message. The phrase "thy fellows who sit before thee" (3:8) probably refers to the ordinary priests with whom Joshua ministered—the priests who served with Joshua in routine daily ministry at the Temple.

"Men wondered at" (3:8) means *men who are a sign*; in other words, types of what is to come. The high priest and his fellow priests were pictures of the High Priest of a new order and the multitude of priests who still serve in that new order.

The Servant

"Behold, I will bring forth my servant, the BRANCH" (3:8). These words and the words that follow move us from the day of Zechariah, Joshua, and Zerubbabel through the centuries to the coming Redeemer of Israel. *Servant* and *branch* are two well-known words for the Messiah in Scripture.

The Book of Isaiah uses the words *my servant* many times. Beginning with Isaiah 42, we find these words used repeatedly as glorious announcements of the coming Messiah: "Behold my servant, whom I uphold; mine elect, in whom my soul delighteth; I have put my Spirit upon him; he shall bring forth justice to the nations" (Isa. 42:1); "Behold, my servant shall deal prudently; he shall be exalted and extolled, and be very high" (Isa. 52:13); "He shall see of the travail of his soul, and shall be satisfied; by his knowledge shall my righteous servant justify many; for he shall bear their iniquities" (Isa. 53:11).

Zechariah, like his predecessor Isaiah, saw the solution to the problem of how sinners can be brought into favor with a holy and righteous God. The righteous servant of God would bear the iniquities of sinners. No animal could bear them, only the righteous one sent from God. The word *servant* also speaks of the humiliation of the Messiah (Isa. 52:13-53:12).

The term *my servant* is used in combination here with another Messianic title, *the Branch*. Isaiah, Jeremiah, and Zechariah all used this title for the Messiah (Isa. 4:2; Jer. 23:5; 33:15; Zech. 6:12). This term connects the Messiah to Israel (Zech. 6:12) and to the line of David (Isa. 11:1). He would be of the line of David according to the flesh, the branch grown from the root of David.

The Stone

> For, behold, the stone that I have laid before Joshua; upon one stone shall be seven eyes; behold, I will engrave the engraving of it, saith the LORD of hosts (3:9a).

Near the climax of the vision in Zechariah 3 is a difficult portion that has sent commentators scrambling in search of a correct interpretation.

The name *stone* has been applied to the Messiah by many. In Daniel the stone is said to be "cut out without hands" (Dan. 2:34) and is declared to destroy the Gentile world powers and establish His kingdom, which shall never be destroyed (Dan. 2:44-45). Psalm 118:22 and 23 state, "The stone which the builders [Israel] refused is become the head of the corner. This is the LORD's doing; it is marvelous in our eyes." Of this same stone we read, "Therefore thus saith the Lord GOD, Behold, I lay in Zion for a foundation a stone, a tested stone, a precious cornerstone, a sure foundation; he that believeth shall not make haste" (Isa. 28:16).

The stone is definitely the Messiah Jesus. When anyone truly believes in Him, He becomes his or her rock of salvation. Although the Jewish people have rejected this stone, He remains the precious cornerstone. In the words of the Apostle Peter,

If so be ye have tasted that the Lord is gracious; To whom, coming as unto a living stone, disallowed indeed of men but chosen of God, and precious, Ye also, as living stones, are built up a spiritual house, an holy priesthood, to offer up spiritual sacrifices, acceptable to God by Jesus Christ. Wherefore also it is contained in the scripture, Behold, I lay in Zion a chief cornerstone, elect, precious; and he that believeth on him shall not be confounded. Unto you, therefore, who believe he is precious, but unto them who are disobedient, the stone which the builders disallowed, the same is made the head of the corner, And a stone of stumbling, and a rock of offense, even to them who stumble at the word, being disobedient; whereunto also they were appointed. But ye are a chosen generation, a royal priesthood, an holy nation, a people of his own, that ye should show forth the praises of him who hath called you out of darkness into his marvelous light (1 Pet. 2:3-9).

Israel's Iniquity Finally Removed

Verse 10 is the climactic portion of the vision, for here we have revelation about the day that many in Israel have longed for but have not yet found. All the sacrifices and rituals of the Old Testament anticipated this day of national redemption.

When will that day be? Has it happened yet? No, it has not happened yet, but it will happen in one literal day. Zechariah pointed us to that day when he declared,

> And it shall come to pass, in that day, that I will seek to destroy all
> the nations that come against Jerusalem. And I will pour upon the
> house of David, and upon the inhabitants of Jerusalem, the Spirit of
> grace and of supplications; and they shall look upon me whom they
> have pierced, and they shall mourn for him, as one mourneth for his
> only son, and shall be in bitterness for him, as one that is in bitterness
> for his firstborn (Zech 12:9-10).

This passage clearly sets forth the fact that Israel will at long last
recognize her Messiah and receive Him. She will deeply mourn for
having rejected Him for so long.

But on which specific day will this occur? It will be at the Second
Coming of Christ, when He returns in His Shekinah glory to set up His
millennial reign on the earth—indeed, in Jerusalem, in the midst of His
chosen people.

Israel's Peace at Last

> In that day, saith the LORD of hosts, shall ye call every man his
> neighbor under the vine and under the fig tree (3:10).

Sitting under the vine and fig tree is an Old Testament way of
expressing peace. When the Messiah returns to earth, He will finally
bring the peace Jewry has sought since the time of Abraham. Their
much-used word, "Shalom," speaks of peace. Peace will finally arrive
when Jesus the Messiah-King returns to the earth. The Jewish remnant
will acknowledge Him, and the iniquity of the land will be removed in
one literal 24-hour day.

The fourth vision of Zechariah thus has moved from a degraded high
priest representing Israel, the sinful nation, to a time when the nation
turns to the Messiah.

As we have seen, Zechariah 3 contains a tremendous challenge, and
there are spiritual principles here that we can ill afford to ignore.
Children of God should heed the commands given to the high priest in
verse 8. We must walk in His ways in all that we do because our Lord
has done so much for us. And although we can never repay the debt
we owe Him, we are called to live and serve Him in purity and
faithfulness.

Furthermore, if you do not know what it is to have trusted Christ,
you are much like the high priest clothed with filthy garments. But Jesus

can forgive your sins today and give you spotless new clothes in exchange for your dirty, sin-covered ones.

ENDNOTES

[1]Feinberg, Dr. Charles, *God Remembers, A Study of Zechariah* (Portland, Oregon: Multnomah Press, 1965), p 45.

ZECHARIAH 4

Vision Five: Israel as God's Shining Light

Since the day the Lord created Israel, His desire has been that she be the repository of His Word as well as the light that would take the message of that Word to all people. Because of her sin, she failed at this task. In fact, the events of the Book of Zechariah took place shortly after Israel's return from the 70-year Babylonian captivity into which God had sent her as a chastisement for her disobedience. The remnant who had returned to their homeland still wondered if the Lord had forsaken them.

The first four visions given to Zechariah offered some hope. The Lord promised to choose Jerusalem as His own city. He promised to remove and destroy the enemies of Israel. Jerusalem would be very great, dwelling in a peace that the Lord promised would come. Zechariah's fourth vision involved the cleansing of Joshua the high priest, indicating that a day is coming when that nation and people will be forgiven and cleansed.

However, the purpose for which God chose Israel—to be the shining light to the nations—had not yet been accomplished. There was still a question to be answered: Can Israel become the shining light God purposed her to be? The fifth vision provided the answer and, in the process, dealt with their immediate need to rebuild the Temple.

The Vision of the Golden Lampstand

Zechariah was awakened by an angel with a question for the weary prophet: "What seest thou?" (v. 2).

Zechariah saw a golden lampstand—a seven-branched candelabra, similar to the one in the holy place of the Temple. The description is consistent with a major theme of the book, the rebuilding of Israel's national house of worship.

The candelabra was modeled after the salvia plant found in the Sinai Peninsula, sometimes called the menorah plant. In the Temple, the menorah provided the only source of light in the holy place. Because no natural illumination ever entered the holy place, the light of the menorah was believed to represent the light of God. Within the inner chamber, the holy of holies, the Shekinah glory glowed above the mercy seat.

Above and perhaps a bit behind the menorah was a bowl that functioned as a receptacle in which to store the oil for the lampstand. Olive oil flowed from this reservoir to supply the individual lamps.

From that bowl emerged "seven pipes to the seven lamps" (4:2b). Commentators offer two explanations. Some hold that there was one pipe from the bowl to each lamp. Others believe that there were seven pipes to each lamp. This view, promoted by scholars David Baron and Charles Feinberg, is based on their translation of the original language, which, they believe, points to seven pipes to each lamp, the Lord thereby signifying a sufficient and abundant supply of oil. Such construction would ensure that the lamps would never run dry of fuel.

Standing on each side of the lampstand were two olive trees, which provided an inexhaustible supply of oil for the bowl and menorah. Interestingly, an ancient Jewish tradition says that only berries from the tops of the great olive trees were suitable for the menorah. The berries from the mid and lower sections of the trees were believed to produce an inferior grade of oil.[1]

Zechariah, his mind in a quandary over what he had seen, was again questioned by the angel: "What are these, my lord? . . . Knowest thou not what these are? And I said, No, my lord" (4:4-5). Verses 11 and 12 make it clear that the wondering prophet needed more information about the two olive trees. "What are these two olive branches which, through the two golden pipes, empty the golden oil out of themselves?" (4:12).

By My Spirit

Then he answered and spoke unto me, saying, This is the word of the LORD unto Zerubbabel, saying, Not by might, nor by power, but by my Spirit, saith the LORD of hosts (4:6).

The last portion of verse 6 is often quoted, but frequently out of context. It is often appealed to when God's people realize that they cannot accomplish certain things in their own strength. And while the statement is certainly applicable to such a situation, several major points of interpretation must be considered to derive its full meaning.

First, the statement is addressed to Zerubbabel, and its meaning must, therefore, be related to verse 7, which pictures Zerubbabel as the great Temple builder.

Second, *might*, in the original language, has the connotation of *the strength of many*. *Power*, on the other hand, gives the idea of *the strength of one mighty person or leader*. This conveys the idea that the restoration of Israel, both in the day of Zechariah and in the future glorious day of the Messiah, would not be accomplished by a great host of armies or by one great human leader. Instead, it would be accomplished by the power of the Holy Spirit.

Third, we understand, of course, that the primary interpretation deals with the rebuilding of the Temple, which was to be accomplished by Zerubbabel. Verse 7 indicates that God would enable him to complete this task and set the headstone of the Temple. The headstone is the final stone used in the construction of a building.

In verse 7 the question is asked, "Who art thou, O great mountain?" The mountain does not represent the Persian Empire, nor Sanballat, who, as Nehemiah documented, hindered the Jews as much as he possibly could. Rather, it represents all the obstacles and hindrances to completing the Temple in the time of Zechariah and Zerubbabel.

God promised that the Spirit of the Lord would remove every obstacle standing in the way of the Temple's completion. Thus, the mountain of problems before the builders would be leveled as if it were a plain (4:7). This would enable Zerubbabel and his fellow workers to complete the task and place the capstone as the people cried out with shouts of joy, "Grace, grace unto it" (4:7). Their shout of "Grace" projected an understanding that God had not forsaken them after all. He was still firmly in control.

God's Promises Fulfilled

Moreover, the word of the LORD came unto me, saying, The hands of Zerubbabel have laid the foundation of this house; his hands shall also finish it, and thou shalt know that the LORD of hosts hath sent me unto you (4:8-9).

The pronoun *me* at the conclusion of verse 9 obviously refers to the angel of the Lord, who we believe is none other than the preincarnate Christ—a fact that should cause believers today to rejoice with even more enthusiasm than did the people of Zechariah's time. With their limited perception, Zechariah's peers could not understand all the implications of this promise. But beyond the immediate reconstruction of the Temple, perhaps we can see the implications of a larger future fulfillment, for this *me* is the one who will bring together all the plans God has for Israel that are yet to be fulfilled. Ultimately, He will cause the millennial Temple, of which Ezekiel spoke, to be built. Reconciled Israel and the Gentile nations will worship the Messiah at this magnificent sanctuary. The details of this Temple are not given by Zechariah but have been carefully described in Ezekiel 40 and following.

The Temple of Zechariah's day was to be much smaller and far less ornate than Solomon's Temple. It also paled when compared to Herod's construction, present in Jesus' day, or the stunning edifice described by Ezekiel. As a result, there were those among the people who despised this small Temple and were not hesitant to complain about it. This was particularly true of those who had seen the splendid Temple of Solomon.

The Lord responded to their expressed disdain through the Prophet Haggai: "Who is left among you that saw this house in its first glory? And how do ye see it now? Is it not in your eyes in comparison with it as nothing? Yet now be strong, O Zerubbabel, saith the LORD; and be strong, O Joshua, son of Jehozadak, the high priest; and be strong, all ye people of the land, saith the LORD, and work; for I am with you, saith the LORD of hosts" (Hag. 2:3-4). In Zechariah, these complainers were addressed through a pointed question: "For who hath despised the day of small things?" (4:10). They were challenged not to evaluate their new house of worship by its lack of magnificence, but rather to see it for its spiritual significance.

As we have seen, the smaller foundation of the Temple had been laid 18 years earlier. Opposition, however, had caused the work to cease. Now the Lord promised that the Temple would soon be completed as the Jewish people were led by His Spirit and obstacles were removed. No one was to complain about its small size and lack of grandeur because this work was of God. It was exactly what He wanted.

There is an important lesson here for contemporary believers because we, at times, fall prey to the same problem. Size and success are often equated: small in size equals little success. As was true in Zechariah's day, such a basis of evaluation manifests a failure to understand God's true purposes and can lead to serious consequences.

A few years back I had a friend in the ministry who became caught up in the idea that success was directly related to large numbers. He accepted a philosophy of ministry taught by certain groups that concluded that worthy ministries must always be growing by leaps and bounds. Although his church was, in fact, a growing, sound work, he became discouraged because he did not feel it was big enough. My friend became so driven by a sense of failure that he took his own life. This is an extreme example, to be sure, but one from which we can certainly learn. Despising the day of small things can be devastating.

At the heart of verse 10 we find the words, "For they shall rejoice, and shall see the plummet [plumb line] in the hand of Zerubbabel with those seven." For years the *building superintendent*, Zerubbabel, had been waiting to return to the most important project of his life. Now the people would see him, plumb line in hand, doing the work that the Lord had called and equipped him to do. It would indeed be a cause for rejoicing.

Zechariah 3:9 mentions seven eyes engraved on one stone. Here we read of them again: "they are the eyes of the LORD, which run to and fro through the whole earth" (4:10b). These eyes were previously depicted as facets of stone, and from them we learn that the eyes of God look over the entire earth. Nothing, now or ever in the future, escapes His view.

The Completion of the Final Work

Zechariah still had some unanswered questions about this vision. "What are these two olive trees . . . ?" (4:11), and "What are these two olive branches which, through the two golden pipes, empty the golden oil out of themselves?" (4:12).

"These are the two anointed ones," he was told, "that stand by the Lord of the whole earth" (4:14). The two pipes (or conduits) mentioned in verse 12, through which the oil flowed, were made of gold. The candlesticks themselves were made of gold, and, although the text does not explicitly state, it is safe to assume that the two bowls were made of gold as well. Undoubtedly there is significance to the fact that golden oil flowed through golden conduits to golden bowls, then through golden pipes to golden candlesticks or lampstands.

Gold often speaks of deity in the Scriptures. Further, the Hebrew word for *anointed ones* is *the sons of oil* or *those characterized by oil*. Although not every Jewish prophet was anointed with oil, both the high priests and kings of Israel were.

The Two Olive Branches

> And I answered again, and said unto him, What are these two olive branches which, through the two golden pipes, empty the golden oil out of themselves? And he answered me and said, Knowest thou not what these are? And I said, No, my lord. Then said he, These are the two anointed ones, that stand by the Lord of the whole earth (4:12-14).

The two olive branches are a new concept. In the passage introducing the vision (4:1-7), no mention was made of the two olive branches. Verse 12, however, states that the oil went through them as well as through the pipes. It is as if Zechariah had just noticed them.

Commentators have concluded that these olive branches unquestionably are symbolic of living beings. In all probability, these living people were Joshua and Zerubbabel, who represented the offices of high priest and king. Each of these offices prefigured the coming Messiah. Joshua is clearly defined as the high priest in Zechariah 3. Although Zerubbabel never ruled as king or was anointed king, he was the leader of his people at that time, and we can conclude that he had a right to the throne of David because He was actually of David's line. These personages therefore provide an answer for the question of verse 12 concerning the identity of the two olive branches: They represent the high priest and the king of Israel. Priests and kings were always anointed with oil, a ceremony not ascribed to prophets.

This is an amazing image! Israel's great high priest and king are declared to be anointed by God "with the oil of gladness above thy fellows" (Ps. 45:7). They are also said to "stand by the Lord of the whole earth" (4:14). In these portrayals we find instruction about the work of the Messiah, for this is exactly what is taught in Hebrews 9:24 about Jesus. He, as our High Priest, is at this very moment interceding in the presence of God on behalf of believers. This same Jesus is also

Israel's coming King. These two offices converge in one person—the Messiah.

Additionally, we read in Revelation 11:4 of the two witnesses who are said to be "the two olive trees, and the two lampstands standing before the God of the earth." Their responsibility is to bear witness of the Messiah, who will first come to destroy the wicked nations and then become both the worldwide sovereign and the High Priest of the redeemed nation of Israel.

The message of this fifth vision was undoubtedly an encouragement to the people of Zechariah's day. The Temple would be rebuilt along with the city of Jerusalem. But, far more important, Israel as a nation would eventually know forgiveness of her sins and fulfill the purpose for which she was created, for one day God Himself will say to the sons of Abraham, Isaac, and Jacob, "Israel, my glory" (Isa. 46:13).

The fixtures in this vision were made of gold, the metal that symbolically represents deity. Combined with other elements of the vision, this sets forth a marvelous picture of Israel's coming Messiah and His glorious millennial position of King-Priest.

Jesus Christ will be the channel through which the oil (Holy Spirit) will flow to Israel. He is the deity represented by the gold, and through Him will flow all that Israel needs to be God's testimony to the world during His millennial reign. The nation of Israel will be as "a brand plucked out of the fire" (3:2), cleansed and forgiven by a divine act and filled with the Spirit of God.

The pattern is always the same. The Lord plucks sinners from the fire, cleanses and forgives them, and, by the power of His Holy Spirit, enables them to be His shining light in a sin-darkened world.

In summary, great truths are presented in the fourth and fifth visions. God can bless Israel spiritually only when, in the future, her sins are forgiven and she walks with the Lord. Israel can be the light God intended her to be only after she experiences forgiveness and the power of the Holy Spirit flows through her. When the Messiah-Jesus returns, He will be the means of blessing to Israel, and she, in turn, will become the source of blessing to the world that God intended her to be.

ZECHARIAH 5

Unfinished Business

Although the truths presented in the first five visions offered comfort and encouragement to that little band of returnees from the Babylonian captivity, some important questions remained unanswered. Namely, was the Lord God really just and fair? Would God allow Gentile nations to continue persecuting Israel? Would there ever be a day of reckoning for them?

Zechariah's three concluding visions, recorded in chapters 5 and 6, provide the answers. The thrust of these visions shifts from consolation to judgment; from Israel to "the whole earth" (5:3). Before the Lord could ultimately bless Israel, it would be necessary to deal with sins and sinners. Inasmuch as a holy God cannot bear to look upon evil (Hab. 1:13), He cannot give total victory until the sin problem is resolved.

The next two visions are so closely connected in thought that some commentators take them to be a single vision. They are definitely connected in concept and even in meaning but appear to be separate visions because of the phrase "goeth forth" (5:3, 5, 6) found in each vision.

Vision Six: God Removes Sinners

The Flying Scroll

The prophet saw a huge flying scroll, approximately 15 by 30 feet. This is the same size as the holy place in the Tabernacle and the porch of Solomon's Temple (Ex. 26:15-25; 1 Ki. 6:3). This scroll was unrolled so that it could be measured. The mind's eye sees something like a flying carpet out of "The Arabian Nights." This was not a carpet, however, but a scroll that was used to carry a written message.

The scroll, when completely unrolled, had writing on both sides (5:3). The writing on the scroll apparently was the Mosaic law. The middle commandment from the second tablet of the Mosaic law was visible on one side of the scroll: "Thou shalt not steal." It represented sins against mankind. On the other side, in the same position, was the commandment against swearing, a sin against God. According to the ancient rabbis, the flying scroll was understood to be a reference to the Torah (Gitten 60b. Soncino Talmud, p. 283).

The flying scroll symbolized the curse on Israel for failing to keep the whole law. Because these two commandments were representative of all the commandments of God, the Lord was communicating through the prophet that all sin will be judged, whether it be against God or mankind. This judgment covered the whole earth, probably speaking of the land of Israel, because the law had been given only to the Jewish people.

Sinners will be cut off: "Then said he unto me, This is the curse that goeth forth over the face of the whole earth; for every one that stealeth shall be cut off as on this side according to it; and every one that sweareth shall be cut off as on that side according to it" (v. 3). The Hebrew word for *cut off* has the connotation of *purged* or *cleaned out*. Final fulfillment of this purging will come in the time just prior to the establishment of the messianic or Millennial Kingdom.

The judgment is sure and complete and extends over the whole land against all the inhabitants. "I will bring it forth, saith the LORD of hosts" (5:4). Judgment will come swiftly and harshly. At present, God's judgment of sin often comes slowly. In fact, some wicked and sinful people never seem to be judged but are allowed to continue in their sin. A day is coming, however, when Jesus Christ will return to the earth and search out all sinners. They will then experience the severity of God's judgment. When that judgment begins to fall, people will flee to the hills to escape. Revelation 6:15 to 17 describes the fate of those who have rejected Christ: "And the kings of the earth, and the great men, and the rich men, and the chief captains, and the mighty men, and every slave, and every free man, hid themselves in the dens and in the rocks of the mountains, And said to the mountains and rocks, Fall on us, and hide us from the face of him that sitteth on the throne, and from the wrath of the Lamb; For the great day of his wrath is come, and who shall be able to stand?"

God's judgment will "enter into the house of the thief, and into the house of him that sweareth falsely by my name" (5:4). The law will be the standard for God's wrath, and there will be a *cutting off*. The meaning of this is difficult to ascertain, but the same Hebrew word is used in Isaiah 3:26 of a city that is totally wiped out.

A man's home is said to be his castle—a place where he can find safety, peace, and comfort. But in this passage, God's judgment enters the dwelling, right into a man's *stronghold*. The strong walls of a transgressor's home cannot keep God's judgment out.

We also see that the judgment of the Lord will remain in the house. It will not just touch the place and depart but will remain there until everything is completely consumed (5:4).

A fascinating picture of the process is presented in the destruction of a house occupied by lepers. Leprosy, used in Scripture as a representation of sin, brings a similar fate to a home. Leviticus 14:45 says of a leper's house, "And he shall break down the house, its stones, and its timber, and all the mortar of the house, and he shall carry them forth out of the city into an unclean place."

Verses 1 to 4 likely have some application to Zechariah's day. They could refer to the Babylonian deportees who, having returned to Jerusalem, withheld some of their tithes from the Lord (Neh. 13:10; Mal. 3:8). By so doing, they stole from God by not giving to Him all that was His due. In a larger sense, however, the passage seems to apply to the end times. Separation of the wicked from the righteous will take place when the iniquity of the land is removed.

Zechariah's vision of sins removed from the earth clearly projects God's hatred for sin. And while people today choose to mock the concepts of sin and subsequent judgment, it does not minimize or negate the solemn consequences revealed to the prophet.

We can be grateful, however, that even though we are all sinners, God sent His Son and "hath made him, who knew no sin, to be sin for us, that we might be made the righteousness of God in him" (2 Cor. 5:21). Because the judgment for sin was placed on Christ, we can be set free by faith in His finished work at Calvary and revel in the grace bestowed on those who believe. "For by grace are ye saved through faith; and that not of yourselves, it is the gift of God—Not of works, lest any man should boast" (Eph. 2:8-9).

Vision Seven: God Removes the Sin System

One major area remained with which the Lord had to reckon—the world system of sin, which had infiltrated the nation and adversely impacted the chosen people. It was a problem picked up in Babylon. Although they had survived the exile, a significant number of Babylonish ways returned to the promised land with them.

The world's first highly developed system of sin—with its pride, commercial greed, ecclesiastical wickedness, and idolatry—originated in Babylon. God had already afflicted that city, as recorded in Genesis 11. But although He confounded the language and scattered the people abroad, the wicked system born in Babylon not only remained but spread with the people as they moved into other lands.

The Ephah

Then the angel who talked with me went forth, and said unto me, Lift up now thine eyes, and see what is this that goeth forth. And I said, What is it? And he said, This is an ephah that goeth forth. He said, moreover, This is their resemblance through all the earth. And, behold, there was lifted up a talent of lead; and this is a woman that sitteth in the midst of the ephah (5:5-7).

Zechariah saw an ephah, which was the largest dry measure available in the Middle East. It held 1.05 bushels of grain. When the prophet first saw the ephah, either he did not recognize what it was or his question was asked for the benefit of future generations.

Inside the ephah Zechariah saw something strange. When the lid was lifted, sitting in the middle of it was a woman called "wickedness" (5:8). "And, behold, there was lifted up a talent of lead" (5:7). This weight of lead, over 120 pounds, was placed on the ephah to serve as a lid or covering for the vessel so that the woman would be trapped inside.

As the vision continued to unfold, Zechariah saw two women come forward, each having wings like the wings of a stork. The wind was lifting their wings. These two women picked up the ephah, with the woman "wickedness" sealed inside, and carried it back to Shinar, the area of Babylon, the very area where all the types of wickedness mentioned earlier had originated. The woman was, in fact, being taken back home (5:9-11), where a house was to be built for her.

This vision is unquestionably a picture of wickedness. It depicts, as it were, sins accumulating like single grains filling the largest available measure. These sins were so numerous that they were heaped up. Sin was no longer a small thing.

Sin was symbolized by the woman sitting inside the ephah. The word *woman* is often used in prophetic Scripture to show religious evil (Rev. 2:20; 17:1-7). Verse 8 clearly states that this woman represents wickedness, especially the wickedness that will culminate in the end times. She depicts the apostate religious system that will reach its zenith at the end of the church age, climaxing during the Tribulation period, when apostate religion will be joined with the godless, commercial Babylonian system. Just as in ancient Babylon, a mammoth materialistic system will develop. This time, however, it will encompass the entire globe.

Returning to Zechariah's day, we must remember that the Jewish people had recently returned from Babylon after nearly 70 years in captivity. The Babylonian system had indeed begun to rub off on them. This vision was to remind them of the condition carried from the captivity; they had been permanently infected by the evil system. It was at this point that many turned from a simple pastoral life to commercialism, trade, and materialism.

Zechariah's contemporary, Haggai, cried out against their transgression: "Then came the word of the LORD by Haggai, the prophet, saying, Is it time for you, O ye, to dwell in your paneled houses, and this house [the Temple] to lie waste? Now, therefore, thus saith the LORD of hosts: Consider your ways" (Hag. 1:3-5). He was forced to speak out against the people, for they were so involved with their own business that they let the Lord's house lie in ruins for 18 years. The sin of idolatry had been overcome by their captivity, but now they had become captive to a new system, secular materialism—actually idolatry of another kind.

The woman "wickedness" was imprisoned, and a talent of lead was put on top of the ephah. Then the two women with wind in their wings took her away, back to Babylon. Wickedness was finally returned home as the Lord judged the earth. This act is symbolic of the Lord's removing sin from the earth, back to its beginning, as it will be destroyed by the Messiah at His coming.

We can learn many lessons from this vision. Wickedness will be destroyed. People involved in wickedness will also be destroyed. Above all else is a great lesson concerning materialism. We cannot serve both

God and mammon. The great materialistic system of this world is not of God, and it will be destroyed. Our goal in life should be to honor the Lord, not to get all we can out of life. The things of this world are completely worthless and will all be carried away some day, and those who live only for this world and its goods will be left with nothing.

ZECHARIAH 6

Vision Eight: The Judgment of the Nations

A casual reading of the eighth vision seen by Zechariah reveals that it concerns four horses, four chariots, and two mountains of brass. This vision is related to Zechariah's first vision of four horses dispatched by the rider on the red horse, who was shown to be the Messiah. In this final vision, the angelic riders are reported to have traveled among the nations to determine their relationship with Israel. The nations were declared to be peaceful and at rest.

Chapter 6 offers an entirely new perspective—one of action. The four chariots symbolize vehicles of divine judgment. In the first vision, after reconnoitering and scouting, they were standing still. In the eighth vision they moved, advancing toward God's final judgment of the nations.

In chapters 1 to 4, as the visions unfolded, God's plan for Jerusalem and His chosen people the Jews was revealed. The Temple would be rebuilt, and eventually the Jewish people would be cleansed and become a reflection of God's light in the world. In chapter 5 God's judgment and punishment fell on sinners and sin. In this final vision, the Lord demonstrated His final judgment against the Gentile nations of the world. When the events of the vision are completed in the end times, the world will be prepared for the coming of the Messiah to rule the earth. This is portrayed in symbolic form with the crowning of Joshua the high priest.

Mountains of Brass

And I turned, and lifted up mine eyes, and looked and, behold, there came four chariots out from between two mountains; and the mountains were mountains of bronze (6:1).

This vision showed not only horses and chariots but two mountains of bronze or brass from between which emerged the war chariots. Brass is used in Scripture as a symbol of judgment. An illustration of this is found in Revelation 1:15 to 16, where Christ's feet of brass are declared to be ready to stamp out judgment on the earth. Most Bible scholars believe that the two mountains spoken of in Zechariah 6 are the Mount of Olives and either Mount Moriah or Mount Zion. In either case, between these mountains is a major valley, the Kidron.

The vision of Zechariah 6 depicts angelic hosts, horsemen, and chariots thundering down the Kidron Valley, bringing the judgment of the Lord on the nations. This will occur at the conclusion of the Battle of Armageddon when the Lord returns in triumph. The details are in precise agreement with the writings of other Old Testament prophets, who speak of a climactic battle taking place in the Valley of Jehoshaphat (Heb., *Jehovah judges*). No location in the Bible is actually named the Valley of Jehoshaphat; however, many Bible scholars believe that it is the Kidron Valley, renamed in the last days. The Scriptures could well be speaking of the valley Jesus will create when He splits the Mount of Olives at His return (Zech. 14:4-5).

The Horses

The horses pulling the chariots are the same colors as those in Zechariah's first vision recorded in chapter 1. They also resemble in color, as well as in function, the horses of Revelation 6. It is apparent that importance is not placed on the color of the animals but on the fact that they were hitched to chariots of war, ready for immediate action to bring God's judgment upon the world. The emphasis here is on the change in direction the judgment is taking; that is, from Israel to the whole earth. The woman "wickedness" being carried out of Israel and back to Babylon symbolizes the fact that God was preparing the entire world for judgment.

As in other visions, Zechariah did not understand the meaning of what he saw. "What are these, my lord?" he asked (6:4). The angel replied, "These are the four spirits of the heavens, which go forth from standing before the Lord of all the earth" (6:5). The number four probably relates to other phrases used in prophecy. For example, the four Gentile kingdoms mentioned in Daniel 2 would touch the nation of Israel. The phrase "the four corners of the earth" (Isa. 11:12) speaks of the whole world. When the vision speaks of "the four spirits of the heavens," it is referring to the entire earth. The judgment is universal.

As is true in Revelation 6, the red horses pulling the first chariot are symbolic of war, the black of famine and death, the white of victory, and the dappled of death brought on by other causes. The horse-drawn chariots may well represent angelic beings sent in different directions as *advance people* to prepare the way for the soon-coming Messiah.

Judgment

The black horses, which represent famine and death, are directed toward the "north country" (6:6). Many of Israel's enemies in history came from the north—some from over the fertile crescent, such as the Babylonians, the Romans, and the Assyrians. Ezekiel 38 also speaks of a fierce enemy allied with other nations that will move against Israel from the north. The white horses follow after the black and symbolize victory. Following the famine and death inflicted on the enemies of Israel, victory will come. The dappled horses head south, toward Egypt, another of Israel's ancient enemies. But none go east or west. The Mediterranean Sea is to the west, and only desert is found to the east. The bay horse is sent throughout the earth.

Victory

After the horses have walked through the Gentile nations and territories, we read, "Behold, these that go toward the north country have quieted my spirit in the north country" (6:8). The horses and chariots are sent specifically north and south, the directions from which Israel's enemies have come. From the south, Egypt was often an enemy, although she never really conquered Israel. From the north, Assyria and Babylon are singled out for special judgment for having overstepped their bounds in punishing the Jewish people. God's angelic messenger goes to the north, and when he returns God's spirit in the north is quieted. Israel's tormentors have been punished, and justice has been restored.

Babylon will receive a special measure of God's wrath, not only because that city exceeded God's intentions in punishing the Jews, but also because she was the birthplace of the wicked, self-centered, materialistic, idolatrous system of commerce and religion. That evil system has permeated the world, and Babylon faces especially severe judgment because of it.

Finally, after eight visions and the promises so wonderfully woven into them, God is ready to bring the program for the earth to its prophesied climax. Sin and sinners have been dealt with, and judgment has fallen. All is prepared for the ushering in of the Messiah. God is ready to intervene in human history for the last time.

Upon hearing this, the discouraged Jewish people who had returned from Babylon must have been ecstatic. God really did care. He cared for them personally as well as for the nation of Israel collectively. He, they could rest assured, was proceeding according to His plan in spite of Satan's opposition.

The Coronation of the King

Zechariah's exciting night of visions was over. The chariots with their horses of various colors were gone. The *God squad* had ridden off into the night. All was quiet as Zechariah pondered what he had seen.

Once the visions were completed, the Lord gave His faithful prophet another word, this time in the form of a symbolic act. Zechariah was told of an event to take place in the morning. The symbolic meaning of this act would put the crowning touch on all that had taken place in the eight visions. It revealed the coronation of the King who would rule over the earth. To assure that the prophet did not miss the message, God used a ceremony Zechariah was familiar with to teach a much-needed truth.

Following the banishment of evil from the earth, a King will be crowned as a worldwide ruler. His majesty is declared by several events and acts soon to take place. The setting is prophetic, for it starts out typically: "And the word of the LORD came unto me, saying" (6:9). Zechariah 7:4 and 8 and 8:1 contain the same phraseology as they announce God's great prophetic plans: "Then came the word of the LORD of hosts unto me, saying . . . And the word of the LORD came unto Zechariah, saying . . . Again the word of the LORD of hosts came to me, saying."

The Circumstances

Zechariah was told to accept the gifts of silver and gold that would be brought by three exiles returning from Babylon. This caravan carried gifts from Heldai, Tobijah, and Jedaiah. In all probability they were very spiritual men, for their names are God-honoring. On the day that the men arrived at the home of Joseph ben Zephaniah, the prophet was told to be there to receive gifts they had brought for the construction of the Temple.

> And the word of the LORD came unto me, saying, Take of them of the captivity, even of Heldai, of Tobijah, and of Jedaiah, who are come from Babylon, and come the same day, and go into the house of Josiah, the son of Zephaniah. Then take silver and gold, and make crowns, and set them upon the head of Joshua, the son of Jehozadak, the high priest (6:9-11).

This event has a far deeper meaning than meets the eye. After being prepared all night by the succession of visions, the prophet saw an event that eclipsed them all—the Messiah crowned King-Priest in the Millennial Kingdom. The gifts brought to him by Gentiles picture the great number of gifts that will be given in the future to build the great and glorious Millennial Temple.

The Crown

Zechariah was to take the gifts brought from Babylon and fashion a crown. The King James translation says "crowns," but it is apparently one crown of combined silver and gold. The distinguishing feature of this passage is the identity of the one on whom the crown was to be placed. It was to be placed on the head of Joshua the high priest. High priests did not wear crowns. God had decreed the attire for the high priest's head to be a turban. Furthermore, the high priest never served as king. The priestly and kingly offices were always separate and distinct. In fact, King David sinned when he entered the Tabernacle and ate the showbread, which was not lawful for him to do (Mt. 12:3-4). As king, he was forbidden to function as a priest.

In light of this distinction, we also must remember an incident recorded in Zechariah 3. Joshua the high priest represented Israel as he stood clothed in filthy garments. He was cleansed by a divine touch and given clean clothing, and a clean turban was set upon his head. Just as

Joshua was a symbol of Israel cleansed, placing a crown on Joshua,
rather than a turban, is symbolic of a day yet future when the Messiah
Jesus will be crowned both High Priest and King as He begins His
millennial reign. This crowning of Joshua therefore was far-reaching
in its symbolic significance.

The Call

Zechariah was instructed to speak certain words to Joshua:

> Behold, the man whose name is THE BRANCH; and he shall grow up
> out of his place, and he shall build the temple of the LORD; Even he
> shall build the temple of the LORD; and he shall bear the glory, and
> shall sit and rule upon his throne; and he shall be a priest upon his
> throne; and the counsel of peace shall be between them both (6:12-13).

This is an amazing passage of Scripture. Although Zechariah was
speaking to Joshua the high priest, his words reached far beyond
Joshua's time. We know this for several reasons. First, the one of whom
the prophet spoke would build the Temple of the Lord. Joshua the high
priest never did this; Zerubbabel did. Second, Joshua was never "the
Branch." Finally, Joshua never bore the glory but, rather, died in
insignificance. Consequently, the crowning of Joshua was to typify one
far greater than he. "The Branch" is a title for the Messiah given by
Zechariah (3:8; 6:12), Isaiah (4:2), and Jeremiah (23:5; 33:15) and is
clearly the Messiah.

The climax of the first six chapters of the Book of Zechariah is found
in the dual office of high priest and king in one person. However, Jesus'
priesthood will be different from Joshua's and will not be modeled after
the Aaronic priesthood but, rather, after another—the order of Melchizedek. Hebrews 5:6, quoting Psalm 110:4, says of Christ, "Thou
art a priest forever after the order of Melchizedek."

The Capstone

The crown to be made would honor Helem, Tobijah, Jedaiah, and
Hen (or Josiah), who had given the materials to make it. They would
not be given the honor of wearing it, however, for the crown was to be
placed in the Temple and left there. According to Jewish tradition, this
crown was hung in a window at the very top of the Temple as a reminder

of God's promises regarding the coming of an eternal King-Priest who would rule over the earth. All the visions of Zechariah, as well as the Word of the Lord given to him in chapter 6, point prophetically toward the ultimate coronation of the Messiah King-Priest. This event will be the consummation of all Jewish hopes and aspirations. With the crowning of the Messiah, sin and unrepentant sinners will have been destroyed, and the curse upon the earth will have been removed. The Messiah will rule over the entire world, and creation will rejoice and cry out, Victory at last!

ZECHARIAH 7

Ritual Replaces Reality

Ritualism means nothing to God unless an inward spiritual reality produces a response from the heart that is compatible with the Word of God. This is exactly the problem surfacing in Zechariah 7 and 8. The Jewish peoples' appreciation for the significance of important events had deteriorated, and religious observances had turned into lifeless ritual.

A Question of Fasting

Nearly two years had passed since the night Zechariah received the eight visions recorded in the first six chapters (cp. Zech. 1:1 with Zech. 7:1). Not only were the Jewish people expecting God's great future for their city of Jerusalem, but change had begun to take place. The walls of the Temple were going up, and the city itself was experiencing a measure of prosperity again. The Jewish people were no longer down in the Valley of Hinnom looking up with only faint hope for their city. God had begun to keep the promises He had made through the Prophet Zechariah. Discouragement turned to joyful anticipation as the situation improved and they began to move ahead.

A delegation of men, led by Sharezer and Regemmelech, was sent from the town of Bethel. They were instructed to inquire of the priests in Jerusalem if they should continue the fast and observe a day of weeping in the fifth month.

And it came to pass in the fourth year of King Darius, that the word of the LORD came unto Zechariah in the fourth day of the ninth month, even in Chislev, When Bethel had sent unto the house of God Sharezer and Regemmelech, and their men, to pray before the LORD, And to speak unto the priests who were in the house of the LORD of hosts, and to the prophets, saying, Should I weep in the fifth month, separating myself, as I have done these so many years? (7:1-3).

Apparently when the captivity had come nearly 90 years before, the Jews had established a number of days of fasting to commemorate some of their national calamities. These fast days included the following:

1. A fast in the the fourth month to commemorate the final breaching of the walls of Jerusalem by the Babylonians.

2. A fast in the fifth month to remember the destruction of the Temple.

3. A fast in the seventh month to remember the murder of Gedaliah, the governor of Jerusalem, placed in power by Nebuchadnezzar after the final deportation of the Jews.

4. A fast in the tenth month to memorialize the beginning of the siege of Jerusalem.

The delegation had a reasonable question: Was it necessary to continue all this ritual? After all, the Jews were back in control of Jerusalem; therefore, these observances had lost their meaning. What had once moved them to tears no longer had any effect on them, and, quite frankly, they were bored with the routine. In fact, what had once been full of meaning was now no more than empty ritual.

The Instruction

We have no record of the priests answering the question of the delegation from Bethel. But the Lord gave His answer through a message delivered by the Prophet Zechariah. The answer came in the form of more questions and instructions that went far beyond the issue of whether or not to continue certain fast days. He not only answered the official delegation from Bethel but provided the necessary directive for the entire nation.

Zechariah's instruction to the people came in the form of a message from the Lord, which called into question their very motives. "Speak unto all the people of the land, and to the priests, saying, When ye fasted and mourned in the fifth and seventh month, even those seventy years, did ye at all fast unto me, even to me? And when ye did eat, and when ye did drink, did not ye eat for yourselves, and drink for yourselves?" (7:5-6). When you, He asked, observe feast days, are they for your enjoyment or in appreciation for what the Lord has done?

In other words, God was asking, Where do I fit into your rituals? It was evident that the Lord had no part in them. The fast days were merely exercises in recalling their past calamities. As a matter of fact, the Lord never instituted these fasts or feasts in the first place, nor was He remembered in the observance of them.

Verse 7 provides the key to understanding this issue: "Should ye not hear the words which the LORD hath cried by the former prophets, when Jerusalem was inhabited and in prosperity, and its cities round about it, when men inhabited the Negev and the Shephelah?"

Zechariah reminded the people that if they had listened to the Word of God given by the former prophets—Isaiah, Jeremiah, Joel, Amos, and Micah—they never would have gone into captivity. Those tragic events would never have come to pass. Had they obeyed God's Word, there would have been no calamities to remember and thus no need for the fasts. The conclusion is very simple: The people should have been listening to the prophets rather than going through their meaningless rituals.

Inexcusable Disobedience

God had given past generations specific commands about how to obey and please Him. They are summarized very briefly in verses 9 and 10: "Thus speaketh the LORD of hosts, saying, Execute true judgment, and show mercy and compassions, every man to his brother; And oppress not the widow, nor the fatherless, the sojourner, nor the poor; and let none of you imagine evil against his brother in your heart."

The Jewish people were to practice truth. Furthermore, they were to be fair and impartial. They were also to exercise kindness and consideration, without taking advantage of the helpless or conjuring up evil against other people. What the prophet wrote here is the essence of the entire Book of James, which also is summarized in one verse: "Pure religion and undefiled before God and the Father is this: to visit the fatherless and widows in their affliction, and to keep oneself unspotted from the world" (Jas. 1:27).

In spite of God's clear commands and promises of blessings for obedience, their forefathers had refused to listen. They were compared to an ox that would not take the yoke. They refused to hear His Word and possessed hearts as hard as "an adamant stone" (a diamond) [7:12a]. In the process they had been careful to retain their ritual. They went through all the motions of piety, frequented the Temple, observed the holy days, and even added extra ones. In spite of this religious charade, however, they were charged with refusing to listen to the message God had for them.

God's Judgment On Sin

Disobedience to God's Word inevitably results in judgment. Verse 12 states, "therefore came a great wrath from the LORD of hosts." This is the same Lord of hosts who had so many times previously helped the nation of Israel. He had been with them and had fought and won their battles for them. But when the nation turned from obeying His Word, He brought several judgments upon them.

1. Although they cried out in prayer, He would not hear. "So they cried, and I would not hear, saith the LORD of hosts" (7:13b). Why should He listen when they would not listen to Him? The psalmist declared the same message: "If I regard iniquity in my heart, the Lord will not hear me" (Ps. 66:18).

2. They were scattered among the nations, thus losing their homeland. "But I scattered them with a whirlwind among all the nations whom they knew not" (7:14a). This was a direct fulfillment of Deuteronomy 30:1 to 3.

3. The land of milk and honey became desolate. It was denuded of trees and depopulated. "Thus the land was desolate after them, that no man passed through nor returned; for they laid the pleasant land desolate" (7:14b).

As has already been observed, Zechariah 7 contains no direct answer to the question of the delegation regarding the fasts. Zechariah diverted their minds from an almost trivial question to far greater spiritual issues. He longed for them to turn back to God's Word and obey it. The last generation had refused to listen and had suffered the horrible consequences. Learn from your father's mistakes, Zechariah cried out to the people, for he knew all too well what happened when people turned back to the same lifeless ritual that had been their forefathers' undoing. If they had only obeyed the Lord in important matters, the problem of fasts would have been easily disposed of.

We can draw important lessons for life from ancient Israel's failure. Do you ever ask yourself why you do certain things? It is easy to get caught up with ritual and allow spiritual reality to slip into oblivion.

We do things the same old way, never asking why we do what we do. It is therefore easy to slip into a ritualistic style of worship, often forgetting or missing the reality behind it. We must constantly be on guard lest we allow important relationships to become commonplace. It is an easy thing to do. A newly married couple, for example, may appear to be deeply in love, but after a few months of marriage they find that their love has lost its fervor, and they find themselves at a loss to explain what happened.

In spiritual matters, first love and zeal for Christ sometime fade, and, as a result, worship and service become almost drudgery. Under such circumstances, the Lord's table, which should always bring our minds back to Christ and the cross, no longer seems to stir our souls as it once did. Spiritual reality then descends into ritualism.

Thus, God's people can be caught in the satanic trap of going through the motions and succumbing to serving empty ritual. Almost without realizing it, they drift into doing for the sake of doing, rather than obeying God with a warm heart. The Lord wants His children to have tender hearts toward Him. He wants us to trust Him with implicit, simple faith and leap to obey His Word. When true obedience becomes our lifestyle, our lives will be enriched with spiritual blessing. Samuel, when confronting Saul, put it well: "Hath the LORD as great delight in burnt offerings and sacrifices, as in obeying the voice of the LORD? Behold, to obey is better than sacrifice, and to hearken than the fat of rams" (1 Sam. 15:22).

Perhaps we, as the people of Zechariah's day, should send a *delegation to Jerusalem* to determine whether we are involved in mere ritual or spiritual reality in our Christian walk.

ZECHARIAH 8

When Fasting Turns to Feasting

Zechariah 7 records that a delegation was sent to the priests in Jerusalem with instructions to ask questions about keeping the fasts. Should they continue them, along with the weeping they had practiced? The delegation received no direct response, but Zechariah presented them with some questions the Lord had given him. Why were these fasts instituted? Was it because of direct commands from the Lord, or did they institute them for their own reasons?

The Lord's prophet challenged them to listen to the warnings of the earlier prophets. "Should ye not hear the words which the LORD hath cried by the former prophets, when Jerusalem was inhabited and in prosperity . . . ?" (7:7). Because the children of Israel had not listened to those messengers of the Lord, God had no choice but to bring judgment on the nation.

The message was very simple: Why do you come asking about these fasts? If you had listened to the Lord's messengers, you would not have gotten into the present difficulty in the first place. The Lord essentially said through Zechariah, You made your own bed; now lie in it!

Zechariah 8 continues to deal with the same problem but looks at it from a different perspective. God previously dealt with the matter from a negative perspective. In chapter 8 He deals with it from a positive perspective.

Previous Considerations

Again the word of the LORD of hosts came to me, saying, Thus saith the LORD of hosts: I was jealous for Zion with great jealousy, and I was jealous for her with great fury. Thus saith the LORD: I am returned unto Zion, and will dwell in the midst of Jerusalem; and Jerusalem shall be called a city of truth, and the mountain of the LORD of hosts, the holy mountain (8:1-3).

The thoughts build quickly in these three short verses. The message of Zechariah 8 concerns the future glorious day the Lord has planned for Jerusalem. The pendulum is swinging from judgment to blessing. Instead of looking back into the past—when Israel turned to idolatry and forced God to exercise judgment—it relates sights yet unseen. At a future time, during the day of the Lord, Jerusalem will be the center of the earth and will know the fullest blessing of the Lord. He will be there, pouring out His blessings in person.

The Lord declares, "I am returned unto Zion, and will dwell in the midst of Jerusalem" (8:3). This looks back to Zechariah 1:16, where the Lord's promise was identical to the one given in this passage. What a great perspective! A city with the Lord present can only experience blessing. Such a life of blessing is what the Jewish people have longed for through the centuries. Furthermore, Jerusalem will be called "a city of truth" (8:3). This final reality reflects the words of Jesus, who said, "I am the way, the *truth*, and the life" (Jn. 14:6). Before Him no falsehood will be tolerated.

The final portion of verse 3 states that the mountain of the Lord of hosts will be called "the holy mountain." This imagery is taken from two other prophets, Isaiah and Micah. Isaiah 2:2 to 5 presents an extended portion concerning this mountain: "And it shall come to pass in the last days, that the mountain of the LORD's house shall be established in the top of the mountains, and shall be exalted above the hills; and all nations shall flow unto it" (Isa. 2:2). The Prophet Micah wrote,

> But in the last days it shall come to pass, that the mountain of the house of the LORD shall be established in the top of the mountains, and it shall be exalted above the hills, and people shall flow unto it. And many nations shall come, and say, Come, and let us go up to the mountain of the LORD, and to the house of the God of Jacob; and he will teach us of his ways, and we will walk in his paths; for the law shall go forth from Zion, and the word of the LORD from Jerusalem (Mic. 4:1-2).

Jerusalem will surely be the city of truth when Jesus Christ rules and reigns from there, for He is truth. Zechariah enlarged on this as he spoke of the topographical changes that will occur in Jerusalem. At that time the city will be lifted up above all others (Zech. 14:10).

Jerusalem will be the dwelling place of the Lord during the Millennium. It will be lifted up, and from it God's truth will flow to the entire world. A day of glory lies ahead for this city of the Lord!

The People of the New Era

Many nations are deeply concerned about their aging populations. How will their social systems be able to handle them? When the present-day baby boomers grow old, how will the dwindling youthful population be able to support them? Some even go so far as to suggest the practice of euthanasia to lessen the burden of older people on the population. The situation will be very different in the millennial Jerusalem prophesied by Zechariah. This passage gives a biblical description of peace and prosperity. First, longevity or long life will be the order of the day: "Thus saith the LORD of hosts: There shall yet old men and old women dwell in the streets of Jerusalem, and every man with his staff in his hand for very age" (8:4). With sin largely removed from the world, the consequence of early physical death will no longer prevail. As a result, multitudes of people will travel the streets of Jerusalem in safety. These godly people may possibly live the entire length of the Millennium.

At the other end of the spectrum of life are children. A multitude of them will play safely in the streets of the city: "And the streets of the city shall be full of boys and girls playing in the streets of it" (8:5). The millennial passages of the Old Testament contain many references to children. They will play with animals that are now fierce but will then be tame: "And the nursing child shall play on the hole of the asp, and the weaned child shall put his hand on the adder's den. They shall not hurt nor destroy in all my holy mountain; for the earth shall be full of the knowledge of the LORD, as the waters cover the sea" (Isa. 11:8-9).

The people of Zechariah's day were merely a small remnant of Jews. How will this great repopulation by both the elderly and children take place? It will require a large number of people in the childbearing years to produce all these children.

The prophet simply stated that it will be a miracle of God (8:6). With the depleted population of the prophet's day, this seemed impossible. Natural population growth could never accomplish it. But just as God intervened in judgment, He can intervene and bring about a miracle in this respect. This is the message of verses 7 and 8.

The Population Returns

The key to understanding the phenomenal expansion of the population of Jerusalem seems to be wrapped up in two words—*east* and *west*. "Behold, I will save my people" (8:7). The word translated "save" would probably be better understood as *deliver*, as it is often translated in other portions of Scripture.

East and *west* are terms used here to portray a return from all parts of the earth. This passage speaks of a great intercontinental regathering. We know this meaning to be correct, for the Jewish people had not gone to the east and west at that point in their history. They had gone only to Babylon in the captivity some years earlier. Perhaps a few had been assimilated into Assyria even earlier. Geographically these nations were considered to be north of Israel rather than east or west. The Jews never went in those directions until the Roman invasion and the diaspora, more than 500 years after the Book of Zechariah was written. Therefore, based on geography alone, God was not about to deliver His people from the east and west at that time. The deliverance spoken of here would not take place for centuries; indeed, it has not yet come to pass in our day, although it may have begun.

Verse 9 clarifies the point. It not only tells of the deliverance of the Jewish people and their resettlement in Jerusalem but qualifies it further: "and they shall be my people, and I will be their God, in truth and in righteousness" (8:8b). This day of deliverance will occur when the Jewish people turn to the Lord nationally, which can only be at one point in prophetic history—when they recognize the Messiah at His Second Coming. It will be a glorious day for the nation and people of Israel. It is described in Zechariah 12:10, discussed later in this study.

The Prophet's Command

The prophets never gave the promises of blessings in a distant future time without dealing with the problems of the day in which they were living. In other words, prophetic truth always had practical application to the lives of those to whom the prophecy was first given. What would happen 200 or 2,000 years from the day in which the people lived did not really matter a great deal to them because they would not be present to enjoy it. So we often find distant promises mixed with promises of what would shortly come to pass.

The Lord commanded the workers to be strong: "Thus saith the LORD of hosts: Let your hands be strong, ye that hear in these days these words by the mouth of the prophets, who were in the day that the foundation of the house of the LORD of hosts was laid, that the temple might be built" (8:9). He was telling the people of Zechariah's day to get on with the construction of the Temple. The Lord sent this message through both Haggai and Zechariah. Although they faced opposition from the Samaritans, the Arabians, the Ammonites, and the Ashdodites (see Ezra and Nehemiah), who tried to stop them from building the Temple at that time and the wall later, God's people were not to listen to them. They were to get on with the work.

We should also note a major contrast between verses 9 and 10 with the use of the phrases "these days" and "before these days." Before they once again accepted the challenge to build their Temple, the people worked in vain. A man worked his fields as long as he could, yet he received hardly any harvest for his labor: "For before these days there was no hire for man, nor any hire for beast; neither was there any peace to him that went out or came in because of the affliction; for I set all men, every one, against his neighbor" (8:10).

In addition to the futility of their labor, they had no peace. Because of affliction, their lives were in constant turmoil. During this period, foreign nations harassed them and old enemies renewed their attacks. Animosity developed among the people, neighbors became foes, and unrest was widespread. Note how the Lord used economic trials, along with unrest between neighbors and harassment by their enemies, to get their attention. Misunderstandings, hatred, animosity, and all kinds of trouble broke out within the Jewish communities. Troubles and trials came from every direction. But God's command was to build the Temple and go on faithfully with Him. Then He would bless them in every phase of their lives.

Neither the Lord nor mankind has changed. People often drift away from God, and He sometimes has to use very stern measures to draw them back to Himself. So it was in the days before the Temple work resumed.

The Return of Prosperity

In verses 11 to 17 the tone of the prophecy changes completely, and God's grace becomes evident once again. In contrast to the judgment God meted out in the earlier captivity, the prophecy about to be given promises rich blessing and prosperity: "For the seed shall be prosperous; the vine shall give its fruit, and the ground shall give its increase, and the heavens shall give their dew; and I will cause the remnant of this people to possess all these things" (8:12). Once again, the prophecy moves from Zechariah's day to a time still future for the nation of Israel: "And it shall come to pass that, as ye were a curse among the nations, O house of Judah and house of Israel, so will I save you, and ye shall be a blessing; fear not, but let your hands be strong" (8:13).

Some who bear the name *Christian* deny that these blessing passages still apply to Israel and the Jews. Instead of taking the promises literally, they allegorize them and claim these blessings for the church. It is the position of this writer that these and other blessings promised to Israel are real and literal and will be poured out upon God's ancient chosen people in a glorious way during the Millennium. We are never free to negate God's promises to the Jewish people.

"But now I will not be unto the residue of this people as in the former days, saith the LORD of hosts" (8:11). The "former days" refer to the years during which God disciplined the Jewish people. He allowed the Chaldeans to capture Jerusalem, destroy the Temple, denude the land, and carry the survivors into captivity and slavery. The Lord announced in this passage that He will remove His judgment from His people, and they will again experience His blessings.

Actually, a dual fulfillment of prophecy comes out of this rich verse. To the Jews living in the time of the prophet, the message was that they would experience a measure of blessing once again. The verse also sets the stage for far greater future blessings.

Changes in Agricultural Conditions

To understand this short section of Scripture, we must understand to whom it is written. In verse 11 God said He "will not be unto the residue of this people. . . ." In verse 12 He said, "I will cause the remnant of this people . . . ." The Lord was not making promises to everyone. He will deal differently with a remnant of the people. This theme is presented not only here but all through the Scriptures. God has a "remnant theology." What does this mean?

God deals with remnants of people. In the case of Israel, only a remnant of the Jewish people in Babylon returned to the promised land from the captivity. Only a remnant will one day return to the Lord, for the remainder will perish in the Tribulation without turning to Him.

"For the seed shall be prosperous; the vine shall give its fruit, and the ground shall give its increase, and the heavens shall give their dew" (8:12). These descriptions are a fulfillment of the Lord's promises given earlier in other portions of Scripture. Let us look at a few of them. "If ye walk in my statutes, and keep my commandments, and do them, Then I will give you rain in due season, and the land shall yield her increase, and the trees of the field shall yield their fruit" (Lev. 26:3-4). "And the LORD shall make thee plenteous in goods, in the fruit of thy body, and in the fruit of thy cattle, and in the fruit of thy ground, in the land which the LORD swore unto thy fathers to give thee" (Dt. 28:11). "And I will make with them a covenant of peace, and will cause the evil beasts to cease from the land; and they shall dwell safely in the wilderness, and sleep in the woods. And I will make them and the places round about my hill a blessing, and I will cause the shower to come down in its season; there shall be showers of blessing. And the tree of the field shall yield its fruit, and the earth shall yield its increase, and they shall be safe in their land, and shall know that I am the LORD, when I have broken the bars of their yoke, and delivered them out of the hand of those who enslaved them" (Ezek. 34:25-27).

As these portions of Scripture indicate, God in His covenants to Israel has promised agricultural blessings when Israel turns to the Lord. Note again that these promises are only for "the remnant of this people to possess all these things" (8:12b).

As noted earlier in this study, Haggai was a contemporary of Zechariah, and he prophesied similar things: "Therefore, the heavens over you withhold the dew, and the earth withholds her fruit. And I called for a drought upon the land, and upon the mountains, and upon the grain, and upon the new wine, and upon the oil, and upon that which the ground bringeth forth, and upon men, and upon cattle, and upon all the labor of the hands" (Hag. 1:10-11). This was the reason for the lack of crops and other problems (8:10).

The Curse Removed

Not only would God remove the curse put upon their crops, but one day He will remove Israel's plight as a curse among the nations. He will deliver this remnant from their troubles and make them a blessing to the nations of the world.

Another nugget of truth is tucked away in the middle of verse 13. The prophet speaks of both the house of Judah and the house of Israel. The two are brought together again, just as the two sticks (Israel and Judah) were brought together in Ezekiel 37:15 to 28. The kingdom that was divided after Solomon's reign will become a single nation once again.

Reviewing the course of the prophecies given in this chapter, we can see that Zechariah has moved from the building of the Temple in his day to the time when the Lord will take a godly remnant of believing Jews into the millennial reign of Jesus their Messiah. With a few strokes of the pen, this ancient writer has led us through some glorious events.

The Contrast Presented

Continuing with the great future the Lord has prepared for Israel, the passage presents a contrast in order to emphasize what He will do for His people. God promised punishment to their forefathers because of their sins. His wrath increased because they continued to sin, and He would not be turned from judging their persistent transgressions. It came as He said it would. In like manner He has promised to bless Jerusalem, and He will never change His mind about what He has designed for the Jewish people. What He has promised He will bring to pass.

Many today teach that these promises belong only to the church. This cannot be the case because the Lord declares this in two distinct ways. First, "your fathers provoked me to wrath" (8:14). This obviously cannot refer to the church fathers. It must designate the idolatrous generation of their forefathers in the land. Second, the promise of blessing is specifically to Jerusalem and the house of Judah. These statements can never be transferred to the church.

The Commands Given

As God unfolded His plan to do good things to Jerusalem as well as to the house of Judah, He gave them certain commands. "Speak every man the truth to his neighbor; execute the judgment of truth and peace in your gates" (8:16). Truth was to control their lives, and peace was to rule their dealings with their neighbors. No evil was to be devised against the people around them. No evil was to emanate from their hearts in any way to anyone. The Lord detests lying and unrest with neighbors. As God was going to change His attitude toward Israel, so the Jewish people had to change their attitudes toward their neighbors.

The Cessation of the Fasts

Changed attitudes by God and Israel prompted a question: What is the need for all these fasts? There was none. Instead of having fasts to remember all the bad moments in their history, God instructed them to have joyful feasts. In other words, the fasts were to be turned to feasts and occasions of joy. "The fast . . . shall be to the house of Judah joy and gladness, and cheerful feasts; therefore, love the truth and peace" (8:19). The horrors of the fall of Jerusalem, the burning of the Temple, and other calamities would drift into obscurity as joy flooded their hearts through the manifold mercies of the Lord.

The Change in Jerusalem

When these changes take place, the Lord will be ruling from Jerusalem. Multitudes of Gentiles will eagerly travel to Jerusalem to pray and to seek the Lord of hosts. It will be a grand and glorious time.

Gentiles will be drawn to Jerusalem during the Millennium because of God's special favor on the Jewish people. God has a great future in store for Israel, and Gentiles will seek to be associated in any way they can with the Jewish people, believing that some of God's blessings will thus be available to them as well. "In those days it shall come to pass that ten men shall take hold out of all languages of the nations, even shall take hold of the skirt of him that is a Jew, saying, We will go with you; for we have heard that God is with you" (8:23).

Today anti-Semitism continues to raise its ugly head. Its ultimate source, of course, is Satan, who is trying to prevent the fulfillment of

God's promises of future blessing for Israel. When Christ rules, Israel will be the head of the nations and will know the return of God's favor. Jewish people will be revered rather than reviled.

This new condition brings us to the zenith of everything that the Lord set in motion in Zechariah chapter 1. The new state will embody Israel's unique relationship to the Lord Himself and the Gentile nations of the Millennium.

ZECHARIAH 9

Two Kings and Final Victory

An entirely new line of thought is introduced in chapter 9. This is the first of two portions that begin with the words, "The burden of the word of the LORD." The second burden is found in Zechariah 12:1. These two major portions of the book go together.

A burden is usually considered to be something that must be lifted or carried. In Scripture it is often related to a message laid on the heart of a prophet, generally one that he had to *unload* or share. Such burdens were frequently declarations of judgment on a nation or a people. The judgment Zechariah had in mind was on Hadrach, Damascus, and other cities listed in chapter 9.

Before examining the details of this chapter, we must understand the setting and the concepts of the remainder of Zechariah's revelation. Basically, two themes dominate the last six chapters of this book: The rejection of, and then the acceptance of, the shepherd of Israel, and the final downfall of the nations and the setting up of the Messiah's kingdom in the end times.

As the prophecies unfold in this chapter, we must also understand basic principles of prophetic Scripture. The writers often recorded several prophetic truths in the same section. Events of which they wrote may or may not follow chronologically and may contain great leaps in time, sometimes within a single verse. We have some evidence of that prophetic style here.

Another important principle comes into play in this section of the Word of God. Often when the Lord gave a prophecy of end-time events, He also gave various prophecies that will be fulfilled along the way. As we see those prophecies fulfilled, we are reassured that the promises of the end times will be fulfilled as well.

For example, suppose you are taking an automobile trip from New York to Miami. Your goal is Miami, but when you start out you do not see any signs indicating the direction to Miami or telling you how far it is. What you do see are signs telling you the distance to Trenton, Philadelphia, and Baltimore. Although you see no mileage signs for Miami, you know that when you reach Baltimore you are well on your way. Although there will be many signs along the way, you probably will not see one for Miami until you get into Florida, just above Jacksonville. But you will find signs for other cities that you know you must pass on the way to Miami. Signs along the way are reminders that you are progressing toward your ultimate goal, Miami.

So it is with prophetic revelations. Events along the way are revealed in advance and assure us that future promises will also literally come to pass. On the basis of such fulfilled prophecy, we can depend on the fulfillment of that which is promised for the future.

The first burden, in Zechariah 9 through 11, deals with the First Coming of the Messiah. The second burden, in Zechariah 12 to 14, deals with the Second Coming of the Lord.

The First Coming of the Messiah

To prepare his readers for the First Coming of the Lord, the writer referred to the exploits of a great king, Alexander the Great. In so doing, he provided a road map for the coming of the Messiah. Most commentators interpret this portion of Zechariah as showing the judgment of nations. Although I believe they are correct, I also believe that the signs along the way show the tactics of this mighty Greek warrior to point people to the Messiah who was to come.

Furthermore, the name of this world military leader is hidden from view here, as it is in Daniel 2 and 7. From an historical perspective, we can look back and recognize him to indeed be Alexander the Great. Cities alluded to in 9:1 to 6 correspond to Alexander's conquests following the battle of Issus in 333 B.C. Also, as related in verse 8 and to be discussed later, Alexander passed by Jerusalem without attacking the city. This was history written before it occurred during his military campaign in the Middle East. Alexander marched into the Eastern Mediterranean area and took one city after another. The biblical details are amazingly accurate. Alexander's conquest is also a picture of a far greater leader who will come in the end times and conquer this area and the entire world as well. This is confirmed at the conclusion of verse 8, where reference is made to the fact that "no oppressor shall pass through them any more.'' Since many oppressors did pass through after Alexander's adventures in the region, the reference can only be to the coming Messiah, whose presence would assure no further oppressors.

The Move Against Hadrach

Archaeologists are not sure exactly where Hadrach was located. Some believe that it is an ancient city in Syria. However, because "Had" means *sharp* and "Rach" means *soft*, it could mean *the area of the sharp-soft*. The Medes were sharp people and good soldiers, but the Persians who followed them were viewed as soft, and some were even known for their effeminacy. It could well be that the future history of the Medes and Persians is tucked away in this one word. If this is the case, the word would not refer to any one city. The Bible does say "the land of Hadrach" (9:1), which seems to indicate a much larger area than a city.

Furthermore, we learn that judgment also fell upon Damascus, an ancient city now located in Syria. From the earliest times Damascus was an enemy of Israel. Today it is the capital of Syria and still among Israel's most dedicated enemies. After defeating Darius at Issus in 333 B.C., Alexander moved to the Eastern Mediterranean, where he subdued the remainder of the Medo-Persian Empire.

The final portion of verse 1 says, "when the eyes of man, as of all the tribes of Israel, shall be toward the LORD.'' When the Grecian army under Alexander moved into the Middle East, fear swept over the entire area. They had never seen an army move like this one, destroying one city after another. Consequently, the eyes of many turned to the Lord, seeking protection or rescue.

The Move Against Tyre and Sidon

Sidon was a small city, but it was close to Tyre and thus gained its fame by association. The two cities together were the capital of Phoenicia, a country that was home to the famous sea people of the ancient world. The Phoenicians proved to be difficult to conquer when attacked by imperial armies. When Babylon finally conquered them after years of struggle, they relocated their city one-half mile out to sea and built what was considered an impregnable fortress around it. The

Phoenicians believed that no one would be able to conquer them. Wealth was no problem for the people of Tyre. In fact, money flowed so freely that it is said, "Silver was as common as dust and gold as common as the dirt."[1]

The Move was Really by God

The king of Tyre was wicked; in fact, he was possessed by Satan (see Ezek. 28:1-19). The city itself was sodden with depravity. God responded to Tyre's wickedness by using the military prowess of the heathen king Alexander to bring down their vile stronghold. Although other kings, such as Shalmanezer and Nebuchadnezzar, had campaigned against this city in the sea and fought against it for years without success, Alexander took it in about seven months. Using slave labor from the areas he had already conquered, he built a causeway out of the rubble over which his army could reach the city, and Tyre was soon defeated.

A major point must be made here. A prophecy is given in Zechariah 9:4: "Behold, the Lord will cast her out, and he will smite her power in the sea, and she shall be devoured with fire." Ezekiel 28:1 to 8 prophesies much about the king of Tyre. He would be possessed by Satan himself. He would claim to be God, but he and his city would be brought down by strangers from other nations. This was to be literally fulfilled and was, in fact, accomplished by Alexander's forces, as we have seen. It was not Alexander, however, who defeated Tyre and Sidon. Their ruin had been ordained by the Lord; but, as has so often been true, God used a human instrument to accomplish His will.

The passage in Ezekiel goes far beyond the king of Tyre, who, being vile as he was, presents a picture of Satan himself. But God used another vile, heathen king to wipe out Tyre, the city of the wicked king. There is a vital lesson to be drawn from this sequence of events. If God could cause the impregnable city of Tyre to fall to Alexander, He can do much more through His King-Messiah, who will come at a later time. No matter how we appraise the events of human history, the Lord is, after all, in control, and mankind can do nothing to change that fact. This is one of the early signposts along the way to the coming of God's King.

Tyre was smitten, her gold was gone, and the city was destroyed by fire. The Word of God was fulfilled.

The Move Against the Philistines

When the people of the Eastern Mediterranean learned of the fall of Tyre, fear swept through their hearts. If that virtually impregnable fortress could fall and be burned by fire, what lot would befall them with their inferior defenses?

The answer is given in this portion of Scripture: "Ashkelon shall see it, and fear; Gaza also shall see it, and be very sorrowful, and Ekron; for her expectation shall be ashamed; and the king shall perish from Gaza, and Ashkelon shall not be inhabited" (9:5). Psychologically, these Philistine cities were already defeated, even though the military action had not yet taken place.

Philistia had five capital cities. This passage records only four, probably because Gath had become part of Judah by that time. The battle accounts of Alexander record only what took place at Gaza. While the other cities fell, the great stronghold of Gaza held out for five months against the armies of the swiftly moving Greek general. When Gaza finally did surrender, Alexander slaughtered thousands of its citizens and sold the rest into slavery. To demonstrate to other cities that he meant business, he had their King Batis (or Beatis) bound and dragged through the streets by a chariot until little was left of his body.

The phrase "And a bastard shall dwell in Ashdod" (9:6) has been given various explanations. Probably the most accurate is that a mongrel people would dwell there. The proud, arrogant Philistine area, Scripture foretells, would be broken down and reduced to nothing. Furthermore, Zechariah clearly prophesied that the idolatrous practices of the Philistines would be removed. Most of the people would be slain, and those who were spared would turn to the Lord. They would embrace the Jewish religion and be absorbed by the people of Judah, just as the ancient Jebusites were after David conquered Jerusalem.

The Move Against Jerusalem

Alexander, with his massive armies, had passed by Jerusalem on the way south to make war against the Philistine cities. He had demanded that tribute be paid, which Israel's high priest refused to do. With the Philistines on his mind, Alexander and his conquering armies bypassed Jerusalem. Once the Philistine area had been secured, the thought of taking the city returned to the general's mind. His swift-moving military machine would now go up to Jerusalem—or so he thought.

God had something to say about that plan. "I will encamp about mine house because of the army, because of him that passeth by, and because of him that returneth" (9:8a). This is a direct promise from the Lord to be the divine protector of Jerusalem when the Macedonian general returned to defeat the city and destroy God's Temple. The Lord Himself would be the protector of His house.

Let us take a detailed look at how that came about. Alexander had asked for help from the Jewish high priest when he besieged Tyre. Because the high priest refused his request and would not pay tribute money, Alexander determined to return and take vengeance on the high priest, the Jewish people, and Jerusalem. When the high priest learned that Alexander was on his way to attack Jerusalem, he pleaded with the people to turn to God. The entire incident is best explained in the historian Josephus' account of it:

> He therefore ordained that the people should make supplications, and should join him in offering sacrifices to God, whom he besought to protect the nation, and to deliver them from the perils that were coming upon them; whereupon God warned him in a dream, which came upon him after he had offered sacrifice, that he should take courage, and adorn the city, and open the gates; that the rest may appear in white garments, but that he and the priests should meet the king in the habits proper to their order, without the dread of any ill consequences, which the providence of God would prevent. Upon which, when he rose from his sleep, he greatly rejoiced; and declared to all the warning he had received from God. According to which dream he acted entirely, and so waited for the coming of the king.
>
> And when he understood that he was not far from the city, he went out in procession, with the priests and the multitude of its citizens. The procession was venerable, and the manner of it different from that of other nations . . . And when the Phoenicians and the Chaldeans that followed him, thought they should have liberty to plunder the city, and torment the High Priest to death, which the king's displeasure fairly promised them, the very reverse of it happened; for Alexander, when he saw the multitude at a distance, in white garments, while the priests stood clothed with fine linen, and the High Priest in purple and scarlet clothing, with his mitre on his head having the golden plate on which the name of God was engraved, he approached by himself, and adored that name, and first saluted the

High Priest. The Jews also did all together, with one voice, salute
Alexander, and encompass him about: Whereupon the kings of Syria
and the rest were surprised at what Alexander had done, and supposed
him disordered in his mind. However, Parmerio alone went up to
him, and asked him how it came to pass, that when all others adored
him, he should adore the High Priest of the Jews? To whom he
reputed, "I did not adore him, but that God who hath honored him
with that High Priesthood; for I saw this very person in a dream, in
this very habit, when I was at Dios, in Macedonia, who, when I was
considering with myself how I might obtain dominion of Asia,
exhorted me to make no delay, but boldly to pass over the sea thither,
for that he would conduct my army, and would give me the dominion
over the Persians; Whence it is, that having seen no other in that
habit, and now seeing this person in it, and remembering that vision
and the exhortation which I had in my dream, I believe that I bring
this army under the divine conduct, and shall therewith conquer
Darius, and destroy the power of the Persians, and that all things will
succeed according to what is in my own mind."[2]

Josephus also stated that Alexander went into Jerusalem and sacri-
ficed to God in the Temple. The high priest explained to him what
Daniel had prophesied concerning the coming of the Greek empire.
Consequently, Alexander treated the Jews with kindness.

This incident serves as another one of those signs along the road.
The Lord had promised that a great general would come into the Middle
East and conquer various areas, and this was accomplished. Details of
how he would relate to Israel and Jerusalem were literally fulfilled. But
amazing as these events were, there is much more to come.

The Move Against All the Enemies of Jerusalem

And no oppressor shall pass through them any more; for now have I
seen with mine eyes (9:8b).

In the middle of this verse, we take a herculean leap in time. A
promise is made concerning a day when Jerusalem will never again be
oppressed by her enemies. God had protected His people by means of
the heathen general Alexander. But Alexander was insignificant compared with the divine protector who will care for His people forever—
the Messiah.

We have seen in the preceding verses of this chapter how God used
Alexander to rid the Middle East of Persian domination. At the same

time that God used Alexander the Great to accomplish this, He also kept him from causing problems for His people Israel.

We live in a day when nation after nation has turned their backs on the little nation of Israel. Even the United States seems to be wavering in her support for the Jewish state. This is distressing for those believers who love Jewish people and are concerned for the welfare of the nation of Israel. And although we are rightly disturbed and moved to pray daily for the peace of Jerusalem (Ps. 122:6), we should never forget that the Lord is watching over her today, just as He did in the days of Alexander and through the events prophesied in Zechariah 9:1 to 8. "He who keepeth Israel shall neither slumber nor sleep" (Ps. 121:4).

The Story of Israel's Coming King

The Announcement of His Coming

Amazingly, in the midst of the prophecy of a pagan king who would come approximately 150 years later, Zechariah foretold the coming of a king for Israel. He is *the King*, prophesied and long awaited, the King God has always had in mind for His people Israel.

The setting for verse 9 is most unusual. Zechariah had first looked ahead to the days of Alexander. Then, in the middle of verse 8, he looked far down the corridors of time to a day when Jerusalem will never again be oppressed by foreign invaders. Immediately thereafter he spoke of the King of Israel who will make all these thing possible.

Rejoice greatly, O daughter of Zion; shout, O daughter of Jerusalem; behold, thy King cometh unto thee; he is just, and having salvation; lowly, and riding upon an ass, and upon a colt, the foal of an ass (9:9).

The triumphant words "Rejoice greatly, O daughter of Zion; shout, O daughter of Jerusalem; behold, thy King cometh unto thee" caused Israel to rejoice at the prospect of the coming of the Messiah. When the heathen King Alexander had approached the city of Jerusalem, the people faced him with fear and trembling. They were then told that another King was coming. He would be none other than the promised one who, as their Messiah, would truly deliver them. A heathen king would come, as wicked men do, to glorify himself, but their long-promised King would come for the benefit of His beloved people.

The Characteristics of the Coming King

He would come to Israel. In ancient days Israel had wanted a king. Although God promised to be their king, they pleaded to be like the nations around them and serve an earthly king. God, in His permissive will, allowed Saul to be king, followed by another of His choosing, David, the son of Jesse, and many others. But under this succession of human kings, most of whom were wicked, the nation soon became divided and seemed on its way to destruction.

God, on the other hand, had something better planned for Israel. It was His Son, Jesus, of the line of David. He would one day come to His people as their King, to rule and reign forever.

He would come with justice. A great contrast is evident between this King and Alexander (cp. Dt. 32:4). Alexander would violently attack anyone who got in his way. The Messiah would be both the just one and the justifier of many (Isa. 53:11).

He would come with salvation. Whereas Alexander butchered thousands and sold multitudes into slavery, the Messiah-King is to be a Savior to Israel. He will save His people from their sins and give them far more than the promised deliverance from their enemies.

He would be lowly. His humility is another contrast to Alexander, who was a proud and arrogant emperor-general. The Messiah humbled Himself, setting all self-glorification aside. This is best presented in Isaiah 53, where the suffering Messiah is portrayed.

He would come riding on an ass. Void of outward splendor, without pomp and ceremony, the Messiah-King of Israel rode into Jerusalem on the back of the lowliest beast of burden. From the days of Solomon on, no dignitary rode on anything but a strong, well-built white charger. This was another sign of the humility of Israel's King, for no one special would ever come riding on a donkey. But the First Coming of the Messiah was the epitome of humility.

He is none other than Jesus. The New Testament quotes this prophecy of Zechariah 9:9 as a portrayal of the Lord Jesus Christ. Matthew 21:1 to 11 describes the disciples securing the animal on which Jesus rode into Jerusalem on what we traditionally call Palm Sunday. The event was identified as the fulfillment of the prophecy given in Zechariah 9:9.

> And the disciples went, and did as Jesus commanded them, And brought the ass, and the colt, and put on them their clothes, and they set him thereon. And a very great multitude spread their garments in

the way; others cut down branches from the trees, and spread them in the way. And the multitudes that went before, and that followed, cried, saying, Hosanna to the Son of David! Blessed is he that cometh in the name of the Lord! Hosanna in the highest! (Mt. 21:6-9).

His coming would be in sharp contrast to that of the previous king. Alexander the Great was portrayed as entering Jerusalem on a great white charger, whereas the Messiah came in a very lowly manner, seated, as it were, on a donkey.

The Conquest at His Second Coming

Although the Messiah came in lowliness and humility at His First Coming, this will not be true in the future. He will come again as a triumphant ruler who will bring peace to the earth. At that time He will ride a great white horse, the symbol of power and might. Revelation 19:11 to 16 describes the event. Verse 11 declares, "And I saw heaven opened and, behold, a white horse; and he that sat upon him was called Faithful and True, and in righteousness he doth judge and make war." He will not come like Alexander or any other conqueror, but as "KING OF KINGS, AND LORD OF LORDS" (Rev. 19:16). His glorious Second Coming will surpass the coming of any earthly ruler. And with Him will come the true peace men have so fervently sought.

He will bring peace in the north: "And I will cut off the chariot from Ephraim" (9:10a). The name *Ephraim* is representative of the ten tribes to the north, or what is known as the Northern Kingdom. The cutting off of the chariot describes some of the results of the Second Coming of the Messiah. When He comes there will be no need for implements of war, for the tribes of the north will experience perfect peace.

He will bring peace in the south, as indicated by the removal of the war horses from Jerusalem. Her arms will finally be laid down after centuries and even millennia of struggle. Peace—permanent peace— will come at last!

He will bring peace over all the world: "and the battle bow shall be cut off" (9:10b). I believe that this is speaking collectively of the Middle East. The man-made implements of war will be removed from the entire area. Neither in the north nor in the south will there be any need for them. The strife that has lasted for so many centuries in that part of the world will finally cease. How will this peace come, and who will bring it?

Peace will be brought by the Messiah: "and he shall speak peace unto the nations; and his dominion shall be from sea even to sea, and from the river even to the ends of the earth" (9:10c). Again we glimpse the Messiah, His return to the earth, and His rule established. He will provide the final solution to the long-lived Middle East problems and will bring perfect peace to all the nations of the world as well. No nation, person, or group—except the Messiah—will ever bring lasting peace to the Middle East or the world.

As for thee also, by the blood of thy covenant I have sent forth thy prisoners out of the pit in which is no water (9:11).

This verse tells us of a dry cistern, a pit without water, and recalls the pit into which Joseph was cast by his brothers (Gen. 37). That event in Joseph's life pointed to this later historical situation. The Jewish people rejected the Lord and have been, as it were, in a dry pit, separated from God nationally.

The covenant referred to in verse 11 is the blood covenant God cut with Abraham in Genesis 15. God promised the patriarch that a great nation would descend from him, and He sealed that promise with a blood covenant. Abraham was told to slay a heifer, a she-goat, a ram, a pigeon, and a turtledove. The first three animals were split in half and laid on rocks on either side of a walkway, and one bird was laid on each side. Abraham was put into a deep sleep by God so that he could not be a participant in the making of the covenant. What is the significance of this scene? In the culture of that day and place, the normal custom was for the two parties to a covenant to walk between the pieces of the animals. But God did not allow Abraham to be a participant in this covenant. God, as it were, made a covenant with God and vowed to bless that people Himself. He would never break His own word, so the covenant was absolutely secure.

Like Joseph, the Jewish people had been cast into a dry pit or cistern, a place where prisoners were held. They had been, figuratively, in a pit during the Babylonian captivity. However, God had made promises to Abraham, as stated above, and those promises extended to them. Because of the promises of that blood covenant, the Lord had allowed them to return home to Jerusalem after the Babylonian captivity.

Turn to the stronghold, ye prisoners of hope (9:12a).

This call has several meanings. First, it was another call for the Jews remaining in Babylon to return home to Jerusalem. Second, it was a call from the Lord to return to God Himself. Although there would be other interim deliverances, the Lord was looking forward to that final day when Israel as a nation will return to Him. Joel stated, "The LORD also shall roar out of Zion, and utter His voice from Jerusalem, and the heavens and the earth shall shake; but the LORD will be the hope of his people, and the strength of the children of Israel" (Joel 3:16). These words point forward to the Second Coming of Christ, when Israel as a nation will finally turn to Him.

Even today do I declare that I will render double unto thee (9:12b).

The normal laws of inheritance in Israel required that the firstborn son receive a double portion from his father (Dt. 21:17). Because Israel is considered the firstborn among nations, she will receive a double portion from God when she is finally restored to millennial relationship and prominence. All nations will look up to her as the leading nation of the world. What a change that will be!

Another sign is emerging on the road to the ultimate victory promised to Israel. Chapter 9 relates that Alexander the Great was a picture of a far greater and more permanent conqueror. This, of course, was Jesus Christ, who would come at a later time, first as a lowly person and then as King of kings.

Other Scriptures state that during the Tribulation, the man of sin, or the Antichrist, will come. His avowed purpose will be to destroy the Jews, hoping thereby to thwart God's plan for the ages. Part of that plan, as seen previously, is to make Israel the head of the nations.

The Maccabean Struggle with Antiochus

This struggle to throw off pagan bondage is similar in scope to the advent of the Antichrist. The Lord magnificently compared Himself to a warrior using various implements of war to handle the situation for Israel. He used Judah as His bow and Ephraim as His arrow in this conflict. During the Maccabean revolt of 175-163 B.C., Antiochus Epiphanes entered the Temple and desecrated it. The Jews were infuriated by his sacrifice of a pig on the altar of their Temple. Judas

Maccabeus and his sons started a rebellion against Greece because of Antiochus' actions. God raised up an army to fight with them against Greece, and they regained their freedom for a brief time.

God promised in this portion of His Word (9:13) to raise up the sons of Zion and make them "like the sword of a mighty man." The battle would be lightning swift, like the storms that develop in the southern part of Israel. The Lord would be the leader in that battle, bringing victory over Antiochus.

The Ultimate Victory

The victory over Greece points to a day when God will give victory to Israel over all the nations that gather against her. This will take place during the era of the Antichrist, who will once again desecrate the Temple. As God enabled Israel to defeat the Greeks, He will also deliver her from a final satanically inspired enemy, the Antichrist.

At the end of the Tribulation period, the Lord will defend the Jewish people as He has done so many times before. When the Lord was on the side of Jewry, they always won the battle or war, no matter how great the odds. Thus it will be in the future.

The LORD of hosts shall defend them; and they shall devour, and subdue the sling-stones; and they shall drink, and make a noise as through wine; and they shall be filled like bowls, and like the corners of the altar (9:15).

This verse may at first seem difficult to understand, but the overall idea is apparent. Sling-stones are those shot by huge catapults. This verse conveys that even huge rocks shot at Israel will miss their mark, and the conquering army will march over them on their way to victory.

The next phrase speaks of making noise as though intoxicated with wine. The more wine people drink, the more boisterous they become. God's people will know such a great victory that they will become as boisterous with joy and excitement as if they were intoxicated with wine.

Furthermore, so much blood will be spilled that Israel will be like the bowls at the corners of the altar filled with the blood of animals sacrificed there. These terms, which are related to priestly activities, indicate clearly that this is a holy war. They also present a picture of

victory. Just as the Maccabees were victorious against Greece, God
will triumph in the end times against the Antichrist and his forces at
Armageddon.

The Ultimate Salvation of the Shepherd-King

And the LORD, their God, shall save them in that day as the flock of
his people; for they shall be like the stones of a crown, lifted up as
an ensign upon his land (9:16).

Throughout the Scriptures, Israel's Messiah is often depicted as the
Shepherd-King. The phrase "as the flock of his people" (9:16) points
out the shepherd relationship. As the Shepherd, He gives His life for
His sheep. He feeds them and tenderly watches over them. He is said
to "save them in that day." Israel will be regenerated as a nation when
their Shepherd-King comes in His second advent at the end of the
Tribulation period. As King, He will lead them in battle, rule over them,
and destroy their enemies.

Not only will they be saved and delivered from their enemies, they
will be as stones or jewels in a crown. The phrase *lifted up* in Hebrew
means *sparkling*. Those redeemed Sons of Abraham will become
sparkling jewels in the crown of the Shepherd-King, the Messiah of
Israel.

For how great is his goodness, and how great is his beauty! Grain
shall make the young men cheerful, and new wine, the maids (9:17).

The final verse of chapter 9 expresses consummate praise. First, it
speaks of the goodness of the Lord. God, who will have saved the nation
of Israel at the end of the terrible Tribulation, is declared to be good.
Israel will realize that He has kept all of His promises to her. The
Psalmist David declared this three thousand years ago when he said,
"Oh, how great is thy goodness, which thou hast laid up for those who
fear thee, which thou hast wrought for those who trust in thee before
the sons of men" (Ps. 31:19). When Israel experiences her redemption
in the end times, she will finally realize just how good God is.

Second, His "beauty" is declared to be great. Psalm 45 is a messianic
Psalm, and verse 2 states of Him, "Thou art fairer than the children of
men." Isaiah recorded it this way: "Thine eyes shall see the king in
his beauty; they shall behold the land that is very far off" (Isa. 33:17).

About His First Coming, the same writer declared, "and when we shall see him, there is no beauty that we should desire him" (Isa. 53:2b). What a change at His Second Coming! To the redeemed of Israel He will no longer be despised and rejected but declared by them to be both good and beautiful.

Finally, corn and wine are used as symbols of the blessings of the Lord. They will be symbols of prosperity in the millennial period and speak of both the physical and spiritual blessings of that day. Praising the Lord for who He is and what He has done is the abiding attitude of everyone who knows Him.

ENDNOTES

[1]Walvoord and Zuck, *The Bible Knowledge Commentary*, p. 1562, col. 2, paragraph 1.

[2]Flavius Josephus, *The Antiquities of the Jews* (trans. by William Whiston), XI, 8,3-5.

ZECHARIAH 10

The Nation Restored

In the previous chapter we saw the deliverance of the Jews from the waterless pit by means of the blood of the covenant. Chapter 10 begins with the command, "Ask of the LORD rain in the time of the latter rain; so the LORD shall make bright clouds, and give them showers of rain, to every one grass in the field" (10:1).

The "latter rain" is the rain that comes in March and April. These rains are timed appropriately to bring crops to full maturity. It goes without saying that when the rains failed to come at the proper time, Israel had a problem. But the people were instructed to pray, and graciously the Lord promised to hear their cry and provide the needed rain. Grass enough would be produced to feed all their flocks and to fill their fields.

The "latter rain" referred to here and in many other texts relates to ancient Israel but also has a spiritual application. When Israel turned from the Lord, the nation experienced times of spiritual barrenness comparable to the dry pit without water mentioned in the last chapter. When the people returned to the Lord, however, they experienced spiritual "latter rain" such as is spoken of in Hosea 6:3: "Then shall we know, if we follow on to know the LORD; his going forth is prepared as the morning; and he shall come unto us as the rain, as the latter and former rain unto the earth."

The Second Coming of Israel's King

The first two verses of chapter 10 offer a major contrast. Prayer brings God's blessings (v.1), whereas trusting in idols leads only to vanity (v. 2), which brings sorrow and national disaster.

Purveyors of Deception

Idols, diviners, and dreamers abounded in Zechariah's day. These idols were probably the small household gods called "teraphim" mentioned throughout the Old Testament. The diviners trafficked in the occult and told lies to the people. For example, in Jeremiah 37 Zedekiah sought advice from such false prophets. Saul, Israel's first king, consulted the witch at Endor, as recorded in 1 Samuel 28:7-25. In addition to the diviners were dreamers and purveyors of false information.

This phenomenon, which was a problem for Israel in Zechariah's time, will become a major factor in the coming Tribulation period. Second Thessalonians 2:9-12 alludes to such deception.

Because of the deceit of false counselors during the Tribulation period, the Jewish people will wander as a flock without a shepherd. Indeed, there will be few good shepherds during "the time of Jacob's trouble" (Jer. 30:7). The people will be sorely "troubled" (10:2) [perhaps this would be better translated *afflicted*].

As we would expect, God's anger will be directed against the false shepherds, the so-called leaders of Israel, and against the "goats," the Gentile rulers allied with the Antichrist in the Tribulation period.

The King is from Judah

Mine anger was kindled against the shepherds, and I punished the goats; for the LORD of hosts hath visited his flock, the house of Judah, and hath made them as his majestic horse in the battle (10:3).

In the middle of verse 3 the thought changes. The Lord promises to pour out His blessing on the house of Judah just as He will pour out His judgment on His enemies. His judgment will be felt by those at Armageddon when the Lord visits "his flock, the house of Judah . . . as his majestic horse in the battle" (10:3). God will not only release His people from the oppression of these false leaders but will use Israel to oppose His enemies in the earth's climactic battle.

The name *Judah* is used here to represent the entire nation. The phrase *majestic horse* is a term indicative of the enabling power of God, which will be imparted to the house of Judah at that time.

Previously the Lord had allowed the tyrannical oppression of foreign leaders to control Israel, but Zechariah informs us that the Messiah will come and properly rule Israel. He points this out in several ways, as seen in verse 4.

The Messiah is the Cornerstone

In verse 4 several things come "Out of him." The word *him* refers to Judah, mentioned in verse 3. Out of Judah "came forth the corner," perhaps better called the *cornerstone.*

Isaiah 28 prophesied that the Assyrians would defeat the ten tribes of Israel in the north, also called Ephraim. Beginning in verse 14 Isaiah declared that Ephraim's coming fall was to be a stern warning to Judah, for she too would succumb to her enemies a little more than a hundred years later.

In the middle of this announcement is a unique statement: "Therefore thus saith the Lord GOD, Behold, I lay in Zion for a foundation a stone, a tested stone, a precious cornerstone, a sure foundation; he that believeth shall not make haste" (Isa. 28:16). A similar passage is found in Romans 9:31 to 33: "But Israel, who followed after the law of righteousness, hath not attained to the law of righteousness. Why? Because they sought it not by faith but, as it were, by the works of the law. For they stumbled at that stumbling stone; As it is written, Behold, I lay in Zion a stumbling stone and rock of offense; and whosoever believeth on him shall not be ashamed." Finally, we read, "Wherefore also it is contained in the scripture, Behold, I lay in Zion a chief cornerstone, elect, precious; and he that believeth on him shall not be confounded. Unto you, therefore, who believe he is precious, but unto them who are disobedient, the stone which the builders disallowed, the same is made the head of the corner" (1 Pet. 2:6-7).

Several conclusions can be drawn from these verses. First, this stone is from God. Second, this stone is called by the personal pronouns *he* and *him.* This cornerstone from the Lord is the Messiah, who would come out of Judah.

David Baron, the eminent Jewish commentator, claims that the Temple's safety depends on its foundation. God's own Son, the cornerstone, holds up both the church and the nation of Israel. Where there once was a wall between us, we now have a common cornerstone. Some day, when Israel enters the kingdom, we will enter it along with her. At that time Gentile Christians and redeemed Jews will be indistinguishable. Hebrew Christians will find their places in both walls. It will be a day of solidarity, with Christ as the cornerstone.

The Messiah is the Nail

"Out of him the nail" (10:4) is an expression laden with meaning that brings interesting insights about the Messiah. The word for *nail* usually refers to a *tent pin* or *stake*. It is also used for the peg that was fastened on the center post of a tent, on which all valuables were hung. In the ancient world the wealth of the entire family often hung on it. We remember the incident with Laban, Jacob, and Rachel. Laban had robbed Jacob again and again. Rachel and Leah, Laban's daughters and Jacob's wives, spoke to him saying, "Is there yet any portion or inheritance for us in our father's house? Are we not counted of him as strangers? For he hath sold us, and hath quite devoured also our money" (Gen. 31:14-15). So Rachel stole the teraphim, or idols, off the nail in Laban's tent. This nail was the one driven into the center post of the tent, upon which all the glory (the teraphim) hung.

Isaiah 22 sheds more light on the imagery of the nail. In verse 20 Eliakim is mentioned. He was to be the overseer of the government—the one, like the nail, upon whom all the glory of God was to hang (Isa. 22:24). But eventually he would be cut down, and everything that depended (hung) on him would fall as well (Isa. 22:25).

In contrast, this portion of Scripture also contains a promise concerning the coming of the Messiah, the one who is sure and certain and will never fail. "And the key of the house of David will I lay upon his shoulder; so he shall open, and none shall shut; and he shall shut, and none shall open. And I will fasten him like a nail in a sure place; and he shall be for a glorious throne to his father's house. And they shall hang upon him all the glory of his father's house" (Isa. 22:22-24a).

This is a marvelous picture of the Messiah Jesus coming to rule and reign over the earth. All the glory of God will hang on Him. This truth looks ahead to the day when He will rule not only over His Father's house (Israel) but over all the governments of the world as well.

The Messiah is the Battle Bow

The battle bow out of Judah signifies that Christ is a warrior, the conquering King who will deliver Israel. Because of Him, every

oppressor will finally depart from Judah. When the Messiah reigns, the
land that has known terrible conflict through the ages will be delivered
and will experience the peace the Jewish people have always sought.
As we have seen, the Messiah is depicted in verse 4 in a threefold
way. He is the cornerstone, the nail, and the battle bow. His coming
will cure Israel's long-standing spiritual blindness and will end all the
oppression she has known.

Victory at the Second Coming

As Armageddon draws to its horrible climax, something amazing
will happen to the troops of Israel: They will be enabled by the Lord
to have strength far beyond what is considered normal. "In that day
shall the LORD defend the inhabitants of Jerusalem; and he that is feeble
among them at that day shall be like David; and the house of David
shall be like God, like the angel of the LORD before them" (Zech. 12:8).
Armed with the power of God, Israel will face her enemies "like mighty
men, who tread down their enemies in the mire of the streets in the
battle . . . because the LORD is with them, and the riders on horses shall
be confounded" (10:5).

The Reinstatement of Israel

And I will strengthen the house of Judah, and I will save the house
of Joseph, and I will bring them again to place them; for I have mercy
upon them, and they shall be as though I had not cast them off; for I
am the LORD, their God, and will hear them (10:6).

The terms *house of Judah* and *house of Joseph* indicate that victory
and reinstatement are promised to all Israel, both the northern and
southern kingdoms. The nation will no longer be divided. This also
fulfills the promise of Ezekiel 37:15 and following that the two
kingdoms will finally be joined together once again.

The Lord will reinstate the nation and people. As God pours out His
mercy on them, they will be fully restored, as if the Lord had never
cast them off. God will hear their cries and prayers once again. As Paul
wrote in Romans 11:23 to 24, the natural olive branch of Israel will be
grafted back into the olive tree again. That will be a glorious day indeed!

Rejoicing

And they of Ephraim shall be like a mighty man, and their heart shall rejoice as through wine; yea, their children shall see it, and be glad; their heart shall rejoice in the LORD (10:7).

When the Lord does these wonderful things for Israel in the future, there will be cause for great rejoicing. The people will be as ecstatic as if they were drunk with wine. The verse states clearly that their rejoicing will be in the Lord. He will be the cause of this future happy day for His people Israel.

Scripture also points out that "their children shall see it, and be glad" (10:7b). It will be the day for which they have all longed, a day of promise known even to the children.

Restoration

In verse 6 the Lord promised, "I will bring them again to place them," and in verse 8 He stated, "I will hiss for them, and gather them." This regathering was promised all through the Old Testament Scriptures. However, the Lord Himself announced what will happen. *Hiss* would probably be better translated *whistle*, which alludes to the signal a shepherd gives to regather his scattered flock. God will signal to the Jewish people who are scattered throughout the world, and they will return home.

Why will the Messiah whistle and the Jewish people eagerly respond? It becomes clear in the middle of verse 8: "for I have redeemed them." This regathering will be possible because of the terrible price the Messiah paid for them when He came the first time and went to Calvary on their behalf. What a glorious message! It reminds us of the day when believers will be gathered to Christ at the Rapture. We have great cause for rejoicing in both cases.

The last part of verse 8 introduces the subject of the remainder of chapter 10: "they shall increase as they have increased." When the Jewish people first went to Egypt, there were only 70 souls—Jacob and his sons and their families. Four hundred years later, when they left the land of the pyramids, there were well over two million people in that multitude led by Moses. It would have been a phenomenal increase in population for any people, but it was especially so for people who had spent most of those years in heavy bondage.

The idea is that just prior to the end times and their entrance into the Millennium, a spectacular population explosion will occur among the Jewish people, far surpassing the one that took place during the Egyptian bondage. Even during the past 200 years, in spite of the Holocaust inflicted on them by Nazi Germany, the pogroms in Russia, and persecution by many other people groups, world Jewry has experienced rapid growth. God's chosen people not only endure, they multiply, even in the most difficult circumstances.

Israel Sowed

And I will sow them among the peoples; and they shall remember me in far countries, and they shall live with their children, and turn again (10:9).

The population increase among the Jewish people will happen even while they are *sown* among the nations. The Hebrew word translated *sow* is never used of scattering but always of sowing in a field that has been prepared to receive seed. When seed is sown in a field and grows, it increases; likewise, when the Jews are *sown* among the nations, they increase.

Israel will eventually remember her God, even while she is scattered among the nations of the world. Their increasing population will eventually cause them to remember the Lord and His covenants with them and their children. They will turn to the Lord and enjoy long-awaited permanent blessings.

Israel Reaped

I will bring them again also out of the land of Egypt, and gather them out of Assyria; and I will bring them into the land of Gilead and Lebanon, and place shall not be found for them (10:10).

The setting of verse 10 is interesting. God promised to bring the Jews out of Egypt and Assyria. These two nations fit into the scriptural picture beautifully. We have already looked at the Egyptian bondage. Assyria was the nation that took Ephraim (the ten tribes of the north) into captivity. Probably Gilead and Lebanon are used here to emphasize the land of the ten tribes of the north.

The last phrase, "and place shall not be found for them," indicates once again that when the Jewish people finally return to their homeland, their numbers will be so large that finding places for them to live will be difficult. Even today, Israel is having a difficult time absorbing the great numbers of Russian and Ethiopian Jews. The waves of immigrants have placed a heavy strain on the resources of the nation.

The last two verses of Zechariah 10 give illustrations from Israel's history that also look toward her prophetic future. When God moved against Egypt at the Red Sea, Egypt's pride was brought down. Her armies died at the miraculous moving of the hand of God. Just as Egypt oppressed the Jews and God had to deal harshly with her, so He will break the pride of Assyria because pride is a sin that God will not allow in either a person or a nation.

Back in their own land, the Lord will strengthen the Jewish people. This probably refers to the outpouring of His Holy Spirit on Israel in the end times (Joel 2:28). Finally, to "walk up and down in his name" (10:12) refers to the freedom and liberty Israel will have in the Millennium. Today believers have this great liberty when they walk in the Spirit.

ZECHARIAH 11

Wrath, Rejection, And Judgment

Wrath On the Land

The first six verses of Zechariah 11 picture such fierce judgment on the land of Israel that the contrast between this chapter and the previous one leaps off the page. The phrases are short, and the words are terse. They speak of great wrath to fall on the land. Although varying views have been presented by a number of commentators, the judgment described here appears to be the judgment on Israel by the Romans in 70 A.D., when they literally denuded the land and left it totally worthless.

The Sweeping Devastation

Open thy doors, O Lebanon, that the fire may devour thy cedars. Wail, fir tree; for the cedar is fallen, because the mighty are spoiled; wail, O ye oaks of Bashan; for the forest of the vintage is come down. There is a voice of the wailing of the shepherds; for their glory is spoiled; a voice of the roaring of young lions; for the pride of the Jordan is spoiled (11:1-3).

This is the poetic style of a lamentation, which contains the technique of personification. For example, neither fir trees nor oaks literally wail. The prophet pictured nature itself mourning deeply over the calamity that had come upon Israel. Because the Jewish people rejected the true Messiah-Shepherd when He came the first time, the Lord allowed the terrible judgment predicted here to fall on the nation. There was no escape when the armies of Rome unleashed their terrible assault on the land and its inhabitants.

The first phrase of verse 1 is almost saying, Let it happen. The fire of judgment would sweep across the land, beginning in the north. The land around Mount Herman would be denuded of its trees. From there, the devastation would move over to the oaks of Bashan, which were in the area across the Jordan River where half the tribe of Manasseh had settled.

Shepherds would wail as their prime grazing land was wiped out. Their glory would be burned, and no place would remain in which to feed their flocks. Even the lions who lived in the thick forests would roar because of lack of food. Wild beasts had moved into the area after the fall of the northern tribes in 722-721 B.C. (2 Ki. 17:25). Evidence apart from the Scriptures indicates that they remained there until at least the 12th century A.D.

The devastation spoken of here would move from north to south, covering the land from one end to the other, including Jerusalem. The nation would wail in grief. Not only would the people fall captive, but the land itself would be utterly destroyed as God used Rome to pour out His wrath on His disobedient people. The pride of the land would be gone for centuries to come.

The Judgment of the People

In the previous three verses, the devastation of the land was described. The next three verses move from the judgment that would fall on the land to the judgment on the people themselves.

The Prophet Zechariah was told to "Feed the flock of the slaughter" (11:4). It could well be that Zechariah was told to act out a drama in front of the people so that they could visualize what God was going to do. This is not an unusual practice in the Word of God. Many people could not read, so prophetic truths were acted out in order that the people might understand the message God was sending through His prophet. For those who could read, the visual message reinforced God's written word.

The word *feed* could also mean to *tend, nurse, care for*, or *lead* the flock. The phrase *flock of slaughter* clearly indicates that this flock was headed for destruction. Even today, animals headed for slaughter are given extra food and care to fatten them up. That is exactly the concept proposed in this verse.

Who was this flock? It was the Jewish people, the nation of Israel. They had departed from the Lord, and God, in His permissive will, would allow the Romans to come and decimate them. Zechariah was told to feed this wayward flock one more time, in the hope that some would heed his message and turn to the Lord. Perhaps this section depicts a final effort by God to spare His covenant people. But they had wandered too far away from Him to even hear His voice.

Two key terms that stand out in verse 5 are "possessors" and "they that sell." Although commentators differ on this point, it appears that these were not the Romans who would come in the future but rather their own religious and political leaders of Zechariah's day—groups like the Pharisees, who exploited the Jews and were leaders in the Jewish rejection of the Messiah. They had become rich at the expense of the Jewish populace and at the same time had been false teachers and faithless leaders.

Finally, in verse 6, God would no longer pity or spare "the inhabitants of the land." He would not only deliver them into the hands of the Romans but would cause such strife among the people that neighbors would begin fighting with each other. They would be delivered into the hand of the king, the Roman Emperor Caesar ("We have no king but Caesar" [Jn. 19:15]).

The Lord also promised that this enemy would crush the Jewish state, including the land. According to the last part of verse 6, the Lord adopted a hands-off policy and would not deliver Israel from the Roman oppressors. Israel had stepped over the line of God's blessing and protection. She pursued her own destruction and refused to listen to the Lord's call.

The situation would be bad enough when foreign invaders came; it was even worse when Israel's own spiritual leaders failed them. But something far worse than that had happened. Because of their sin, God Himself was forced to turn His back on them. Now they were all alone with no one to hear, not even God to whom they belonged. It is a sad day when God has to turn away from His own people. This is an abiding warning to all who turn a deaf ear to the call of the Lord.

The Shepherd with the Staves

In verse 7 Zechariah was again told to "feed the flock of slaughter." It is apparent that he was still acting out an object lesson for the people. In this verse he spoke of the "poor of the flock" or the oppressed. This group could well have been the remnant of true believers who lived in

Israel at the time of Christ's birth—people like Anna, Simeon, Elizabeth, Mary, and Joseph.

Zechariah picked up two staves to act out the part of a shepherd. One was called "Beauty," and the other was called "Bands." In Psalm 23 the shepherd is said to have a "rod" and a "staff," tools to lead and protect the sheep. These tools were given names that symbolized how God had treated the Jewish people. The rod was used to beat off wild beasts. The staff was used to gently lift up sheep that were caught in a thicket or had wandered over the edge of a cliff. The rod was very firm, the staff very gentle.

"Beauty" was a picture of graciousness. God had graciously and tenderly cared for His covenant people. When Jesus was on the earth He was gracious, gentle, loving, and kind to His people. He was meek and humble, even though His people were far from God and the truths of His Word. Our wonderful Lord was certainly a picture of graciousness and compassion at His First Coming.

The second staff is called "Bands," the concept being that of unity—tying or binding together or bringing about a oneness. Jesus always desired that His people be one flock under one shepherd, healing the division that had developed in the nation.

"And I fed the flock" (11:7c). The promise given in the first phrase of verse 7 was repeated as a completed act. Jesus "went about doing good" (Acts 10:38). Just as God promised, He did His best to draw the Jewish people to Himself.

The Shepherd's Impatience

> Three shepherds also I cut off in one month; and my soul loathed them, and their soul also abhorred me (11:8).

Commentators have offered many variant views on this passage; it clearly causes problems of interpretation.

The cutting off of three shepherds is better understood as disowning them. But who are these shepherds? Some believe the passage refers to the cutting off of the prophets, for in the time of Christ there were no prophets, and there had not been one for centuries. Perhaps a better explanation would be that the three shepherds who were disallowed were the priests or religious leaders; the scribes or teachers of the law; and the elders who acted as the civil leaders of the land. Under these

leaders wickedness reached its zenith during the time of Christ. Their
spiritual corruption contributed to the crucifixion of Jesus.

The last part of verse 8 speaks of their utter disdain for Christ, as
well as the fact that Jesus lost His patience with them. This is amplified
through a study the "woes" of Matthew 23. Although Jesus had given
them numerous opportunities, they turned totally away from Him. On
the other hand, the Jewish leaders regarded Jesus with loathing and
disgust.

The Shepherd Abandons Israel

Having lost patience with both the religious leaders and the people
who followed them, the Messiah said, "I will not feed you" (11:9) or
shepherd you. All the tender care Jesus had for Israel was removed.
He literally "gave them up," as in Romans 1:24. Tragedy would now
befall the nation.

Several illustrations are used to depict the spiritual condition of the
people: "that which dieth, let it die; and that which is to be cut off, let
it be cut off; and let the rest eat, every one, the flesh of another" (11:9).
These sheep were in a dying condition, and the Messiah would do
nothing to restrain death from coming: "let it be cut off" (11:9). Christ
turned His people over to the Roman judgment of 70 A.D. Finally He
went so far as to suggest that the rest of the people, in their total rejection
of Him and their vindictiveness toward each other, were devouring one
another, just as Paul described in Galatians 5:15.

What a tragedy! They were judged and given up because of their
rejection of the Messiah. We can learn a powerful lesson from this. We
risk destruction if we turn our backs on the gracious and tender care of
our loving Lord.

Graciousness is Gone

Zechariah took the staff that was in his hand, called "Beauty" or
graciousness, and broke it in pieces. The prophet was told to perform
this act as a sign that the Lord had broken a covenant He had made with
the people. The covenant spoken of here was not one of His basic
covenants with Israel but, rather, a covenant God had made with the
nations. The covenant was this: Although nations would come against
Israel at God's bidding to punish her for her sins, God placed certain

restraints on them. He had set bounds and limits on the length and severity of the oppression. With the breaking of the staff of graciousness, those limits were lifted. God's hand of protection and graciousness for His people was removed. Almost anything could happen because Israel was no longer under God's hand of protection.

The Shepherd's Price

And I said unto them, If ye think good, give me my price; and if not, forbear. So they weighed for my price thirty pieces of silver. And the LORD said unto me, Cast it unto the potter—a lordly price that I was prized at of them. And I took the thirty pieces of silver, and cast them to the potter in the house of the LORD (11:12-13).

Again, the actual interpretation of these two verses is quite difficult, although the prophetic implications are most recognizable and clear. First, the shepherd asked the flock if his ministry was of value to them. If so, how much was it worth? An action and reaction by the people followed, as they considered the entire ministry of the good shepherd. Having been treated horribly, he put the question to Israel, as if his ministry might not have been worth anything to them. It was like saying, If what I have done is worth anything to you, please give me my pay. If you don't think it was worth anything, forget it. Don't bother.

The shepherd, of course, did not really want any pay. Rather, he wanted to make the people aware that even after all he had done for Israel, they wanted little or nothing to do with him. He was totally unworthy and worthless in their sight.

Just as Zechariah in other places acted out a dramatic scene, here he acted out how little his people would value their Messiah when He came. They decided that He was worth 30 pieces of silver, the price of a slave gored by an ox and thus rendered useless (Ex. 21:32). It was an insult, worse than if they had given nothing. This action proved that the Lord was correct in breaking His covenant with the nations (11:10) and allowing them to come against Israel and destroy her in 70 A.D.

The concept of casting the money to the potter is probably an idiom, like, "Throw it to the dogs." The throwing down was done in the house of the Lord and means *get rid of it.*

Of major interest is how the New Testament used this portion of Scripture in regard to the betrayal of Jesus by Judas Iscariot. Matthew 26:14 to 15 records that Judas asked the chief priests what they would give him to betray Jesus. They all agreed on the price of 30 pieces of silver. For that insignificant sum, the Lord's own disciple, Judas Iscariot, who was a thief from the beginning, agreed to betray Jesus into their hands. Although Jesus was the true King of the Jews, He was sold for a few paltry coins. What an insult to the Savior, who was God incarnate.

After Judas had betrayed the Lord, he realized what a heinous act he had committed. To salve his wicked conscience, he returned to the Temple, bringing back the blood-tainted pieces of silver, and threw them down on the ground. The betrayer of Jesus then went out and hanged himself. "And the chief priests took the silver pieces, and said, It is not lawful to put them into the treasury, because it is the price of blood. And they took counsel, and bought with them the potter's field, to bury strangers in" (Mt. 27:6-7). Amazingly, the money Judas received for betraying the Lord was used to purchase the very place where his body was soon to be buried. It could not go back into the Temple treasury and was, as Zechariah prophesied, "Cast . . . unto the potter" (11:13).

One detail needs clarification. Matthew stated that he was referring to what Jeremiah said, when it was actually Zechariah who said it (Mt. 27:9). The first impression is that there might be an error in the Bible, or perhaps Matthew couldn't remember who wrote the passage. Neither is true. The fact is that "Jeremiah stands at the head of the prophetic roll he used, according to the ancient order preserved in numerous Hebrew manuscripts and familiar from Talmudic tradition."[1] In other words, Matthew was referring to prophecy according to the common method of his day, citing the prophet whose name appeared at the beginning of the scroll on which the prophecy was recorded.

Breaking the Staff

> Then I cut asunder mine other staff, even Bands, that I might break the brotherhood between Judah and Israel (11:14).

Zechariah was then called upon to act out another scene, one that would be a most vivid portrayal of God's message to His people. Already the staff representing God's gracious patience with Israel had been broken. Now, after the nation had totally rejected the Messiah, one more act had to be carried out to complete the picture.

The prophet took the other staff in his hands and broke it in pieces. Because of Israel's rejection of the Lord, unity was broken. The bond between Israel and the Lord was destroyed. The prophet's action confirmed symbolically that all relations between the shepherd and his flock were severed. He was saying by this act that God had broken the bonds that held the nation together. Israel would be destroyed and the people scattered abroad throughout many nations for a very long time. Because they refused Him, He turned His back on them nationally. Rome was then free to do as she pleased.

There are several important truths to be learned from this portion of Zechariah.

1. Zechariah was showing that prior to the downfall of the nation, the Messiah would come. He would attempt to "feed the flock of slaughter" (11:7). In other words, the Lord would send His Son to make one more effort to draw Israel to Himself.

2. The leaders of Israel or the "three shepherds"—the priests, scribes, and elders—would totally reject the Messiah. This would leave the Lord no choice but to swiftly cut them off (11:8).

3. A group of the poor would follow Him. Looking back, we can see among that group people like Simeon, Anna, Elizabeth, Mary, and Joseph. The great multitudes of the nation, however, would have nothing to do with Him (Jn. 1:11).

4. The coming Messiah would be betrayed and would be of no more value, in the eyes of His people, than a slave who had been gored by an ox and rendered useless.

5. Because of the rejection of the true Shepherd of Israel, the people and the land were to be given over to death, dispersion, war, destruction, and denuding of the land. Jewry would then, for centuries, become a dispersed and downtrodden people.

Accepting the Foolish Shepherd

Between verses 14 and 15 there is another significant leap in time. It goes from the coming of the Romans in 70 A.D. all the way to the Tribulation period, a time that is still in the future. The Jewish people not only rejected God's true Shepherd in the past, but, sadly, they will accept the "idol shepherd" (11:17)—the Antichrist—in the future. It is amazing that this people will turn to one who will be designed and raised up by Satan to totally destroy them.

The Lord called on Zechariah to act out one more prophecy. He took up the instruments of a foolish and wicked shepherd. The normal instruments of a good shepherd would assist the sheep—a crook, a rod to beat off the enemy, a knife, and a few other utensils. What were the instruments of a foolish shepherd? Some have said that he would not wear the clothes of a shepherd but, rather, some outlandish clothing. Others have said that his only instrument would be a club to beat the sheep. Although it is not clear exactly what his tools would be, we can be assured that they would not benefit the flock.

This passage depicts the wicked shepherd, the Antichrist yet to come. Although he will come on the world scene appearing to bring peace, order, and prosperity, he will soon reveal his true identity. Instead of doing good, he will turn on the Jewish people and use his club to decimate them once again. In spite of all of this, most of the world, and many Jewish people, will be taken in by him. They will have rejected the true Shepherd only to follow after a false one who will bring them only harm.

"I will raise up a shepherd" (11:16). Nothing happens outside of God's plan. God Himself will raise up this foolish shepherd to fulfill His purposes as the time draws near for the true Shepherd's return to rule and reign during the Millennium.

Neglecting Needy Sheep

The sheep are divided into two groups—the needy sheep and the healthy, robust ones. The passage goes on to tell what the wicked shepherd will do to each type of sheep. First, the false shepherd "shall not visit those that are cut off" (11:16). These sheep will be separated from the main part of the flock. They will be cold, helpless, hungry, weak, and in danger of attack from prowling wild beasts. He will not look after them and protect them as a good shepherd.

Second, he will not "seek the young one" (11:16). Anyone who raises animals, whether cattle or sheep, does his best to care for both the mother and the newborn. Years ago, while in the pastorate, we had in our church a very faithful family who raised sheep. The only time of the year they missed services was when their sheep were "lambing." They tenderly assisted in the birth process, especially attending to the new lambs that were born. The family's conduct reflects the proper attitude toward the lambs of the fold. Such will not be true of the false shepherd, for the Antichrist will have no concern for the Jewish people, who are God's children. Through the analogy of sheep, Zechariah depicted the lack of tender care of the young by this worthless shepherd of the end times.

Next, he will not "heal that which is broken" (11:16). Many young sheep break bones as they graze in strange places. A good shepherd tenderly splints the broken leg and even carries the lamb until the leg has healed. This faithless shepherd will simply ignore them.

Destroying the Sheep

Turning to the strong and healthy sheep, the worthless shepherd will not feed the ones that stand still, waiting patiently to be led to green pastures, but instead will let them starve. People living in Zechariah's day seeing a shepherd behave in the way acted out by the prophet would call him a terrible shepherd. No true shepherd would do any of those things.

We are further told that this evil shepherd "shall eat the flesh of the fat, and tear their claws in pieces" (11:16). Not only will this so-called shepherd neglect the needs of the flock, but he will go so far as to destroy the strong sheep and tear them, just as the wolves do. What a horrible picture! He will be so greedy that he will devour the sheep rather than care for them.

All of these actions characterize the coming Antichrist. At first he will look good. For three and one-half years he will seem to care for the Jewish people. Then he will reveal his true nature, and everything will change. With the abomination of desolation (Dan. 9:27) and the setting up of a statue of himself in the rebuilt Temple, he will turn against Israel. The peace covenant he made with the nation will be broken, and he will launch a holocaust greater than any the world has seen. Two thirds of the Jewish people in the land of Israel will perish (Zech. 13:8).

Such will be the work of the wicked shepherd. Yet many in Israel will turn to him. Having rejected the true Shepherd, they will accept this false one, who will bring them nothing but distress and destruction.

The Foolish Shepherd Judged

Woe to the idol shepherd that leaveth the flock! The sword shall be upon his arm, and upon his right eye; his arm shall be completely dried up, and his right eye shall be utterly darkened (11:17).

"Woe!" This word is used many times in the Scriptures at the beginning of a pronouncement of judgment. It is used here to get the people's attention for a prophecy of great importance—the judgment that is coming.

The phrase "The sword shall be upon his arm" deals with the right arm in the Hebrew, which symbolized a man's strength. The verse goes on to say that "his arm shall be completely dried up." A sword will strike the arm and destroy its strength. It will wither, and his power will be gone.

The sword will affect his right eye, which is sometimes used to symbolize intelligence. God's judgment on him will cause him both to become weary physically and to be brought low mentally, even to the point of becoming feebleminded. This wicked shepherd will certainly meet with the judgment of God.

The foolish shepherd will bring terrible suffering to Israel. He will tear into her, desiring to completely destroy her. After a season, however, God will deal with this evil one, bringing judgment on him.

We praise God that He is not yet finished with Israel. At the same time that the Antichrist, the foolish shepherd, is being judged, the Lord will begin to deal with the Jewish people. Chapter 13 describes the fountain of cleansing that will be opened to Israel when she finally looks to the true Messiah for cleansing.

ENDNOTES

[1]Unger, Merrill F., *Zechariah: Prophet of Messiah's Glory*, p. 201.

ZECHARIAH 12

The Future of Jerusalem

Turmoil, trial, heartache, and death seem to be the constant companions of the Jewish people. For centuries Jewry has faced major problems. The Spanish Inquisition, Russian pogroms, and Nazi Holocaust are just a few of the nearly innumerable instances of vilification and violence endured by the Jewish people. After reestablishing their nation once again and going *back home* in 1948, strife and wars have continued to plague the nation. Such distressing circumstances would seem to justify the questions, Has God forgotten us? Will there ever be an end to strife and bloodshed? Will things continue to get worse? Is there any hope?

Chapters 9 through 11 of Zechariah might cause readers to wonder. The Lord promised His King for Israel, but when He came He was rejected by His own. God provided a Shepherd for her, and she would not follow Him. Instead, the people chose to follow false shepherds. Scanning yet future events, we find that Israel will follow one final false shepherd, the Antichrist. With such information at hand, the future appears bleak.

However, in the concluding chapters of Zechariah the picture changes. These chapters introduce a future day when God will remember Israel once again. This visitation will see her delivered from all her enemies. Bloodshed will cease, and Israel's situation will be altered for eternity. The hope of the ages will become a reality when God's Shepherd-King Jesus rules and reigns over His redeemed people.

Provision for Israel

Chapters 12 to 14 are a single unit linked by several key phrases and words that are used repeatedly. For example, the phrases *in that day* and *at that day* are used 16 times, the name *Jerusalem* is used 23 times, and the name of the Lord or other nouns and personal pronouns referring to Him are used 60 times. These chapters present a clear picture identifying a future day when the Lord will do something special for Jerusalem. He has not forgotten her. As stated previously, the very name of the book we are studying, *Zechariah*, means *God remembers*.

The first prophetic burden, recorded in chapters 9 to 11, tells of the Messiah's First Coming, Israel's rejection of the true Messiah, and her acceptance of a false messiah, the Antichrist. The second burden, recorded in chapters 12 to 14, describes His Second Coming and Israel's acceptance of her Messiah-King.

Divine Authority Over Israel

The burden of the word of the LORD for Israel, saith the LORD, who stretcheth forth the heavens, and layeth the foundation of the earth, and formeth the spirit of man within him (12:1).

Strong emphasis is given to the omnipotence of the God of Israel. Before prophesying what was to be accomplished by divinely exercised authority, Zechariah referred to His creative power. God stretched out the heavens, He laid the foundations of the earth, and He made man in His own image. The God who was able to do these things is certainly able to care for Israel. He is totally sovereign in the operation of both heavenly and earthly spheres. "Behold, he who keepeth Israel," the psalmist reminds us, "shall neither slumber nor sleep" (Ps. 121:4). Our omnipotent Lord can and will bring to pass what He promised to Israel.

A Cup of Trembling

Behold, I will make Jerusalem a cup of trembling unto all the peoples round about, when they shall be in the siege both against Judah and against Jerusalem (12:2).

This segment begins by using three images to describe what the Lord will do for Jerusalem in the future. First, He spoke of another day when the city of peace will be besieged by invading armies. He promised on that occasion, however, to make Jerusalem "a cup of trembling" to all the armies that will be gathered against her. What is "a cup of trembling"? The Hebrew word for *cup* used here is *saph*, a word used nowhere else in Scripture. It is a cup from which people drink only intoxicating beverages, and drinking from it causes people to stagger and reel from drunkenness. In the future day spoken of in this passage, the armies of the earth that are gathered against the city of Jerusalem will be, as it were, drinking of the wine goblet of Jerusalem, intoxicated with a fury that will cause them to try to destroy her once and for all.

What Is The "Cup of Trembling"?

To best understand verse 2, we must search two parallel passages. The first is found in Isaiah 51 and the second in Jeremiah 25.

"Awake, awake, stand up, O Jerusalem, which hast drunk at the hand of the LORD the cup of his fury; thou hast drunk the dregs of the cup of trembling, and wrung them out" (Isa. 51:17). This passage declares the "cup of trembling" to be the wrath of God. For generations, Israel had known God's fury. She had repeatedly turned to idolatry and consequently faced severe chastisements from the hand of the Lord. Later in this same passage, the thought changes. The "cup of trembling" remains the same, but it is poured out, not on Israel, but on her enemies. "Thus saith thy Lord, the LORD, and thy God who pleadeth the cause of his people: Behold, I have taken out of thine hand the cup of trembling, even the dregs of the cup of my fury; thou shalt no more drink it again, But I will put it into the hand of those who afflict thee, who have said to thy soul, Bow down, that we may go over; and thou hast laid thy body like the ground, and like the street, to those who went over" (Isa. 51:22-23).

Jeremiah 25 strengthens the point. The Lord said through Jeremiah: "For thus saith the LORD God of Israel unto me, Take the wine cup of this fury at my hand, and cause all the nations, to whom I send thee, to drink it . . . Then took I the cup at the LORD's hand, and made all the nations to drink, unto whom the LORD had sent me . . . And it shall be, if they refuse to take the cup at thine hand to drink, then shalt thou say unto them, Thus saith the LORD of hosts, Ye shall certainly drink" (Jer. 25:15, 17, 28). God will prevail over the nations who oppose Israel. Whether they acknowledge His authority over them or not, they will ultimately do His bidding.

The total concept of this first word picture in chapter 12 is simple: Israel, having suffered repeated outpourings of fury from the Lord, will one day witness that fury removed from her and meted out instead against those nations that have oppressed her. Israel's trials, tribulations, and testings will then be over, and God will be ready to bless her.

Jerusalem Will Be a Burdensome Stone

And in that day will I make Jerusalem a burdensome stone for all peoples; all that burden themselves with it shall be cut in pieces, though all the nations of the earth be gathered together against it (12:3).

The second image concerning Jerusalem is found in verse 3, where it is described as "a burdensome stone," a stone too heavy to lift.

Some years ago, I visited the ancient fortress at Acco (Acre) just north of Haifa on the northern coast of Israel. Inside the huge underground fortress are several courtyards. One had a large pedestal with a round stone displayed on it. The stone was used with a catapult to be hurled at attacking enemies. I was challenged to pick up this large stone. Knowing that it was too heavy to lift, I bent over, pulled in my elbows, and by bending my arms was able to slightly budge the stone on the pedestal. If someone had removed the pedestal, the stone would have fallen on my feet and crushed them.

A day is coming when Jerusalem will become like that stone and will, in fact, fall on all the armies gathered against her. Daniel 2 describes clearly a stone cut without hands that comes crashing down, hits the feet of the image that represents the Gentile world powers, and smashes it to pieces. The stone pictured is Christ, for we are told that it "became a great mountain, and filled the whole earth" (Dan. 2:35).

The stones of Daniel 2 and Zechariah 12:3 are similar, although not exactly the same. Zechariah speaks of the same stone—Christ—crushing all the armies of the world that will be gathered against Jerusalem. Although they will come to destroy the city, they themselves will be wiped out.

One further comment should be made about Zechariah 12:3. The last phrase says, "though all the nations of the earth be gathered together against it." At the end of the Tribulation period, just before the Lord Jesus returns, anti-Semitism will be rampant. Under the leadership of the Antichrist, the whole world will rise up against the Jewish people and Jerusalem. To whom can the Jewish people look? Governments will hate them and send their armies to destroy Jerusalem and its people.

At this juncture, there will be only one direction left for them to look, and that is up. This is exactly what is depicted later in Zechariah 12.

Jerusalem Will Be a Sea of Confusion

In that day, saith the LORD, I will smite every horse with terror, and his rider with madness; and I will open mine eyes upon the house of Judah, and will smite every horse of the peoples with blindness (12:4).

This verse may seem confusing at first reading. To understand it, we must examine it carefully. This third image is centered on horses. The verse speaks of a terrified horse that has gone blind and is therefore frightened and unpredictable. Upon that wild horse is a rider who has himself gone mad.

Blindness and terror, combined with the fact that the rider of the horse so afflicted is mad or crazed, portrays a situation in which utter confusion reigns. So it will be in the closing days of the Tribulation period, when total confusion will overtake the earth. Although we are not yet in the Tribulation period, we must agree that we are living in a world where confusion is increasingly a daily fact of life.

Years ago, while a college student, I was exposed to a terrifying example of the kind of chaos spoken of in Zechariah 12. A horse barn was struck by lightning one night and caught fire. A group of us ran to the scene before the firemen arrived, hoping to lead nearly 50 horses out of the barn to safety in a nearby pasture. The animals were in their stalls and had neither bit nor bridle anywhere near them. Forming groups of rescuers, we tried to walk the horses to safety. But just as we got them almost to the gate of a safe pasture, they became frightened, bolted, and ran back into the blazing barn to their death.

Tucked in the middle of verse 4 is a phrase that seems almost out of place: "I will open mine eyes upon the house of Judah." This statement will be examined in connection with verse 10. Suffice it to say for now that this seems like calm in the midst of a storm.

And the governors of Judah shall say in their heart, The inhabitants of Jerusalem shall be my strength in the LORD of hosts, their God (12:5).

This verse can be difficult to understand, depending on how it is translated. Some take the verse to mean that the leaders of Judah will be inspired by the inhabitants of Jerusalem because they will derive their strength and hope from trusting in the Lord of hosts. Others hold that the verse should be translated with a different emphasis and should read, "the strength of the inhabitants of Jerusalem is in the Lord of hosts [the armies], their God."[1] Regardless of which position we take, we see in this passage the population of southern Israel finally turning to the Lord. This is a consequence of the Lord opening His eyes in grace on the house of Judah (12:4).

The Preservation of Israel

The LORD also shall save the tents of Judah first, that the glory of the house of David and the glory of the inhabitants of Jerusalem do not magnify themselves against Judah (12:7).

A preliminary reading of this verse may leave readers a bit puzzled. When battle comes, we would expect that the well-fortified areas, such as Jerusalem and the surrounding region, would quickly gain the victory. This is not the case, however.

The passage speaks of the areas inhabited by Bedouin tribes, the less populated areas where no armies or military strength are present. God has a very good reason for this plan. If the house of David (usually thought of as a strong military power) or a well-fortified Jerusalem experienced victory first, they would take all the credit for the defeat of the enemy. God will not allow such pride to be served. He alone will win this battle, and the accrued glory will be His. As the Tribulation comes to its climax, the armies of the earth will step into the final battle, seeking ultimate victory over the Jewish nation. At that time a miraculous event will take place. Instead of God allowing the armies of the earth under the Antichrist to defeat the badly decimated Israeli forces in their last-ditch battle, the Lord will directly intervene, and the tide of battle will change very swiftly.

He Did It Before

In that day shall the LORD defend the inhabitants of Jerusalem; and he that is feeble among them at that day shall be like David; and the house of David shall be like God, like the angel of the LORD before them (12:8).

The first portion of this verse, "In that day shall the LORD defend the inhabitants of Jerusalem," is a remarkable statement, but it is nothing new. God has done it before.

During the Assyrian campaign, Jerusalem was besieged for an extended period. Food was so scarce in the city that the Jewish people resorted to desperate measures in order to survive. Animal refuse became an odious alternative to death by starvation. Even the bodies of those who perished were sought for sustenance. In reality, however, their lot was far from hopeless, for Isaiah had a word from the Lord:

> For out of Jerusalem shall go forth a remnant, and they that escape out of Mount Zion; the zeal of the LORD of hosts shall do this. Therefore, thus saith the LORD concerning the king of Assyria, He shall not come into this city, nor shoot an arrow there, nor come before it with shields, nor cast a bank against it. By the way that he came, by the same shall he return, and shall not come into this city, saith the LORD. For I will defend this city to save it for mine own sake, and for my servant David's sake (Isa. 37:32-35).

The extent of God's power to intervene and bring ultimate victory over Sennacherib, king of Assyria, was thus revealed. He "departed, and went and returned, and dwelt at Ninevah" (Isa. 37:37). The reason for the king's hasty departure was the decimation of his forces by the angel of the Lord, who entered the camp of the Assyrians and destroyed 185,000 of his troops.

He Will Do It Again

Just as the Lord intervened against Sennacherib, He will do so again in the future. Those armies were soundly defeated, perhaps merely by a spoken word. Therefore it should not be difficult for believers to understand that when the Lord makes a promise, He can and will carry it out. The next time, however, instead of defeating the army of one king, God will defeat and destroy all the armies of the world.

Not only will the Lord personally defend the inhabitants of Jerusalem, but He will also enable the people living there to be vital participants in both the battle and the ensuing victory. Several illustrations are given to prove this point.

"He that is feeble among them at that day shall be like David" (12:8). Elderly men, ordinarily too weak to go to war, will be strengthened by the Lord so that they are able to fight as well as their war hero, King David, renowned for his many exploits and victories in battle.

The house of David will be so powerful that it will do battle as God Himself did. They will fight as if the angel of the Lord is personally leading them. This, in fact, seems to be the case, for supernatural power and strength will be needed to bring about the spectacular victory promised by the Lord.

Zechariah 12:9 clearly records the Lord's intentions: "And it shall come to pass, in that day, that I will seek to destroy all the nations that come against Jerusalem." Make no mistake about it—although men will be enabled to fight, this victory will be won by the Lord. All the credit will be His.

The Penitence of Israel

For nearly two thousand years the Lord has been dealing with the Jewish people on an individual basis concerning their salvation. As is clearly taught in Romans 11, national Israel has been set aside because of their rejection of the Lord. The wild olive branch—the church—has been grafted in. However, that passage in Romans also speaks of a day coming when the natural branch—Israel—will be grafted back in. Paul wrote that it will be a great day. Zechariah 12:10 to 14 spoke of the very same event, the day when the nation of Israel turns to the Lord.

Grace Poured Out

And I will pour upon the house of David, and upon the inhabitants of Jerusalem, the Spirit of grace and of supplications; and they shall look upon me whom they have pierced, and they shall mourn for him, as one mourneth for his only son, and shall be in bitterness for him, as one that is in bitterness for his firstborn (12:10).

In Zechariah 3:9 the Lord promised to "remove the iniquity of that land in one day." Zechariah 12:10 tells a little more about that promise, stating that Israel will look to Christ, the one they pierced. When this takes place nationally, the nation will mourn as if they had lost their firstborn or only son. Their mourning will be like that of Pharaoh and his subjects on the night the death angel visited Egypt many centuries ago.

Families mourn when loved ones die. Nations have been plunged into mourning at the sudden loss of a leader by assassination or death. Nearly every person alive who has reached a mature age has experienced this problem, in one way or another, but the mourning spoken of in verses 11 to 14 goes far beyond the normal experience of mankind.

The Historical Mourning

In that day shall there be a great mourning in Jerusalem, as the mourning of Hadadrimmon, in the Valley of Megiddon. And the land shall mourn, every family apart; the family of the house of David apart, and their wives apart; the family of the house of Nathan apart, and their wives apart; The family of the house of Levi apart, and their wives apart; the family of Shimei apart, and their wives apart; All the families that remain, every family apart, and their wives apart (12:11-14).

These may seem to be strange words, but they have great significance in the annals of ancient Israel. A great mourning will sweep the land, so great that every family member will weep alone.

I had no comprehension of what this meant until an event took place in my own life. While I was speaking in southern Florida, I received an urgent call from my wife Joan. "My Mom has had cardiac arrest and is not expected to live," she said. Joan was at our home in Charlotte, North Carolina, with our children, while her mother lay dying more than 500 miles to the north. She was deeply troubled.

When I offered to cancel the last meetings and return home immediately, she said, "No, finish the week, and then come home." Very early on Monday morning, I began the drive home. When I arrived at about 6 p.m., Joan simply said "Mom went to be with the Lord at 5 o'clock this morning."

I wept. My heart went out to her, but she did not cry. The next day our family travelled north for the funeral. Joan never shed a tear during the entire experience. Although her tenderness continually showed, she never cried.

After we returned home I questioned her about this because it did not seem to be normal. She finally said, "I cried at the news, weeping the night through. On Saturday and all day Sunday I wept, and again all night. Then at the news of Mom's death I cried all day. When you came home, there were no tears left.'' Perhaps I caught a slight glimpse of what is being described here in the words "and their wives apart.''

"The family of the house of David'' mentioned in verse 12 apparently refers to the royal family. Likewise "the family of the house of Nathan'' probably refers to the prophetic line, "the house of Levi'' to the priestly line, and "the family of Shimei'' to the scribal line. The point is that the entire nation will mourn as never before.

What is the cause of this great mourning by the entire nation? They will finally realize that the one they have rejected for so long is their Messiah—Jesus.

ENDNOTES

[1]Unger, *Zechariah: Prophet of Messiah's Glory* (Zondervan, 1976), p. 211, par. 3.

ZECHARIAH 13

Israel Cleansed

T he previous chapter told of the day when Israel will turn to the Lord. At that time, she will come as an entire nation and will carry the stains from centuries of separation from the Lord. This chapter reveals her cleansing.

The Cleansing Fountain

In that day there shall be a fountain opened to the house of David and to the inhabitants of Jerusalem for sin and for uncleanness (13:1).

When Israel as a nation finally looks upon her Messiah and recognizes who He is, a fountain will open to her to provide forgiveness and cleansing. Her problem has been sin. The sin that forced her into captivity was idolatry. The resolution to her problem is couched in terms of what faced the Jews of Zechariah's day.

The cleansing fountain of verse 1 covers two areas. It will provide cleansing "for sin and uncleanness." The sin had to do with their breaking the first commandment by putting other gods before the Lord. This "uncleanness" could very well refer to the sins that resulted from idolatry and sexual sins. This verse states that forgiveness will be open to the nation.

Cutting Off Idolatry

And it shall come to pass, in that day, saith the LORD of hosts, that I will cut off the names of the idols out of the land, and they shall no more be remembered; and also I will cause the prophets and the unclean spirit to pass out of the land (13:2).

God abhors idolatry. He removed the Shekinah glory from Solomon's Temple when idol worship moved in. He removed Israel and

Judah from the land when idolatry permeated every corner of the country.

In a major sense, Israel learned her lesson about idol worship through the Babylonian captivity. Although this passage refers to a future time, the Lord directed the prophet to use terminology familiar to the people of his day to make a point about major changes in the future.

It is clear that God will remove completely the very essence of the problem of idolatry. He will remove the idols not only from the land but from people's memories as well. Furthermore, the false prophets who led them in idolatry will be gone, as well as the "unclean spirit," the satanic agents behind the idols. When God moves, He will make a clean sweep.

The Claims of the False Prophets

And it shall come to pass, in that day, that the prophets shall be ashamed, every one, of his vision, when he hath prophesied; neither shall they wear a rough garment to deceive (13:4).

Any false prophet who remains in the land after the Messiah's cleansing of Israel will try to hide himself because he will be totally ashamed of what he is and what he has done. To hide their identities, these followers of Satan will wear everyday clothing like other people. Realizing that being discovered will mean immediate death, they will attempt to disguise themselves.

I am no prophet, I am a farmer; for man taught me to keep cattle from my youth (13:5).

Furthermore, they will lie about their occupations. These debauched individuals who have stooped to satanic deceit will continue to follow his ways by continually lying to protect their own lives. However, their lies will be exposed, and they will be incarcerated and put to death.

Cuts in the Hands

And one shall say unto him, What are these wounds in thine hands? Then he shall answer, Those with which I was wounded in the house of my friends (13:6).

Verses 4 and 5 show that false prophets will seek to hide their identity in order not to be slain. The context of verse 6 offers two possible interpretations. The first is that a question is asked of a false prophet, "What are these wounds in thine hands?" The wounds could refer to self-mutilation practiced by the prophets as part of their heathen rituals. The answer comes back, "Those with which I was wounded in the house of my friends."

The second interpretation is that the verse does not refer to the false prophets at all but to another prophet who is yet to come, the Messiah Jesus. The "wounds in thine hands" in that case would refer to the wounds He suffered on the cross of Calvary. His own friend, Judas, had betrayed Him, and His own people had turned their backs on Him, rejecting Him as their Messiah. Nails were driven into His hands and feet, and a Roman spear was thrust into His side. He was wounded in the house of His friends.

Command of the Sword

Awake, O sword, against my shepherd, and against the man who is my fellow, saith the LORD of hosts; smite the shepherd, and the sheep shall be scattered; and I will turn mine hand upon the little ones (13:7).

Verse 7 begins with a command to a sword, indeed a strange way to speak. The sword is told to go "against the man who is my fellow." The word *fellow* conveys the idea of equality with the one who is speaking. The speaker also says the "fellow" is "my shepherd." This can be none other than the Messiah Jesus, the Great Shepherd. This is a call to the sword to go against the Shepherd, the Messiah, and cause His death, which was also prophesied in Isaiah 53 and other places throughout the Scriptures.

As the command continues, the prophecy states that the sheep will be scattered. This is an accurate description of what happened to the disciples—the sheep—after the crucifixion of Jesus. With their leader dead, they lost all hope. They believed that the earthly kingdom they had anticipated would never come. Their situation had changed drastically in a few short days. With no hope, no leadership, and nowhere to go, the disciples began to scatter.

Then a very significant promise is given: "I will turn mine hand upon the little ones." Although initially difficult to understand, it is a beautiful promise once it becomes clear. An illustration can be used to best interpret the turning of the hand. When a parent's hand is stretched out, palm down, a child understands that punishment is coming. The same hand turned over, palm up, is held out in love rather than judgment and offers welcome and comfort to the child. God's message was that He would not forget the young and new believers at Christ's death. He would turn His hand and pour out His blessings on the little group of sheep that would be the nucleus of the New Testament church.

The Suffering of Israel's Remnant

The scene changes completely in verses 8 and 9. We are taken into the Tribulation once again and told of events that the Jewish people will experience at that time.

From this portion of Scripture it is apparent that all the holocausts, pogroms, and inquisitions of the past have been insignificant compared with what is yet to come. With our finite minds we may think that the Jewish people have suffered enough, but here we learn that Satan will make yet another attempt to destroy Israel. This prerecorded suffering results in two significant things: Some will be refined to purity, and the remnant of the Jewish nation remaining after the purification will be brought to the Lord as a whole. Let us examine these verses in detail.

> And it shall come to pass that in all the land, saith the LORD, two parts in it shall be cut off and die; but the third shall be left in it (13:8).

There are two views on the phrase *all the land*. The Hebrew word for *land* is *eretz*. This verse can very definitely refer to *eretz* Israel. If so, it is conveying that two thirds of the Jewish people residing in Israel will die. That would be a tragedy—a great loss of many souls. However, the word *eretz* is also used in a much broader sense in other passages. For example, Genesis 1:1 states that "God created the heaven and the earth." *Eretz* is used there to designate the entire earth.

We cannot say definitively which meaning is intended in verse 8, *eretz* Israel or the entire *eretz* earth. In either case, another holocaust will afflict Jewry, one far worse than any they have known.

> And I will bring the third part through the fire, and will refine them as silver is refined, and will test them as gold is tested; they shall call

on my name, and I will hear them. I will say, It is my people; and
they shall say, The LORD is my God (13:9).

In spite of such decimation of the nation, God has a marvelous plan
for the surviving remnant. He "will refine them as silver is refined,
and will test them as gold is tested" (13:9). Refining metal requires
great heat.

The ore or impure metal is heated to a very high temperature. At a
certain point the impurities separate and can be removed, leaving behind
the pure silver or gold. Israel's Tribulation remnant will be thus refined
to reflect unparalleled beauty and purity.

Reconciled and refined Israel will have called on the name of the
Lord, trusted in the Messiah-Jesus, and been saved. Zechariah 3:9 states
that this will happen in one literal day. When that Jewish remnant is
brought through the testing and is purified, God will call them His
people, and they will say, "The LORD is my God" (13:9c). Reconcili-
ation and restoration of God's chosen people will at last be complete.

ZECHARIAH 14

The Final Deliverance of Jerusalem

Behold, the day of the LORD cometh, and thy spoil shall be divided in the midst of thee. For I will gather all nations against Jerusalem to battle; and the city shall be taken, and the houses rifled, and the women ravished; and half of the city shall go forth into captivity, and the residue of the people shall not be cut off from the city (14:1-2).

There are indications throughout the Book of Zechariah that by the end of the Tribulation period Jerusalem will be in a desperate condition. The armies of the world will have moved against her, and the wrath of God will be in the process of being poured out. Needless to say, Jerusalem will wear the look of a beleaguered city.

Zechariah 12:3 says, "though all the nations of the earth be gathered together against it." This verse reiterates the fact that "I [God] will gather all nations against Jerusalem to battle" (14:2). It will be a horrible day for the Jewish people. The wrath of all nations will be poured out on Jerusalem and its people. What is described so graphically is Satan's final fling in the Tribulation period. For years Israel's enemies have tried to drive her into the Mediterranean, but they have failed repeatedly. This time, however, Jerusalem will be defeated.

This chapter describes in detail the events that will take place in the battle for Jerusalem. Verse 2 states that the city will fall into the hands of the enemy. Houses will be rifled or robbed. Goods owned by the Jewish people will be plundered and taken as the spoil of battle. Women who fail to escape will be ravished or raped. Obviously, the rules of warfare will be forgotten when Satan makes his final assault on the city of the King.

"Half of the city shall go forth into captivity." As in the days of the fall of Jerusalem to Babylon, many of the people will be led away captive.

Scripture indicates that the other half of the people will remain in the still-smoldering ruins of the city. Our imaginations enable us to envision what will happen to them. The enemy troops will feel so secure that they will divide the spoil "in the midst of thee" (v. 1). The normal procedure for an enemy was to gather the spoil from the city, haul it outside the city walls where there was more security, and divide it. This time, however, they will feel so confident in their victory that they will sit in the open within the city and divide what they have taken in battle. The evidence is clear that this will appear to be a humiliating defeat for Jerusalem and its Jewish inhabitants.

The Divine Deliverer

Then shall the LORD go forth, and fight against those nations, as when he fought in the day of battle (14:3).

The emphasis of the passage changes from the defeated nation to the divine deliverer. This event is foretold in several other places in Zechariah, such as 12:8 and 9. It is also alluded to elsewhere in Scripture. The Messiah Himself will go forth and crush the armies assailing Jerusalem.

And his feet shall stand in that day upon the Mount of Olives, which is before Jerusalem on the east, and the Mount of Olives shall cleave in its midst toward the east and toward the west, and there shall be a very great valley; and half of the mountain shall remove toward the north, and half of it toward the south (14:4).

General Douglas MacArthur, upon leaving the Philippines after an American defeat in World War II, said, "I shall return," and he did—this time in victory. When Jesus ascended from the Mount of Olives, He also made a promise to return to the very spot from which he ascended: "Ye men of Galilee, why stand ye gazing up into heaven? This same Jesus, who is taken up from you into heaven, shall so come in like manner as ye have seen him go into heaven" (Acts 1:11). Verse 4 speaks clearly of that return. This is not the Rapture but His Second Coming, when He will return to the earth to rule for a thousand years.

Jesus' feet will literally be planted on the Mount of Olives overlooking the city of Jerusalem. The place of His return is given very specifically—"before Jerusalem on the east." He will actually split the

mountain in two from east to west, forming a valley through which the
Jewish people who are left in the city can flee.

The valley is called "a very great valley." The maps of Israel never
properly identify the Valley of Jehoshaphat, which some think is the
Valley of Megiddo or the Kidron. The name *Jehoshaphat* comes from
two Hebrew words, the first obviously being *Jehovah*. The second
word, *shaphat*, means *to judge*. Could it be that this new valley will be
the Valley of Jehoshaphat?

The Promise of Ultimate Deliverance

And ye shall flee to the valley of the mountains; for the valley of the
mountains shall reach unto Azel; yea, ye shall flee, as ye fled from
before the earthquake in the days of Uzziah, king of Judah; and the
LORD, my God, shall come, and all the saints with thee (14:5).

When the Mount of Olives splits in two, the Jewish people will flee
through the newly created valley, which is said to reach to "Azel"
(14:5). Although it is not certain where Azel is, it could be the Beth-ezel
recorded in Micah 1:11. Sometimes in Scripture when the name of a
place begins with *Beth*, that part of the name is left off. Such might be
the case here.

No record exists in any of the historical books of the Old Testament
regarding the earthquake mentioned. However, the Prophet Amos
mentioned an earthquake of great magnitude (Amos 1:1). It must have
been a huge one, covering a large area, for he dated his writings by it.
Just for the record, large earthquakes in Israel were not uncommon in
ancient days. Evidences of them are still visible in the land.

The annals of Jewish history must have contained records of how the
people fled from the massive destruction of the earth-shattering event.
Zechariah, speaking of the splitting of the Mount of Olives by the
returning Messiah, declared that the people will flee as they fled the
destruction of the earthquake in the days of Uzziah, mentioned above.

"And the LORD, my God, shall come, and all the saints with thee"
(14:5c) is a magnificent statement regarding the Lord's Second Coming.
It is parallel to the description in Revelation 19:11 to 16 of the Lord's
return to the earth to make war and to judge hostile Gentile nations.
The Revelation passage records that the armies that were in heaven
followed with Him.

When Christ returns to the earth to defeat His foes, all the believers in heaven will come with Him to participate in the victory celebration. Nowhere in the Bible are we told that those heavenly armies will do any fighting. The war will already be won. This is the day for which all of creation has groaned for so long (Rom. 8:18-24). In addition to physical deliverance, the earth will finally be set free from the bondage brought about by Satan so long ago.

> And it shall come to pass, in that day, that the light shall not be clear, nor dark, But it shall be one day which shall be known to the LORD, not day, nor night; but it shall come to pass that, at evening time, it shall be light (14:6-7).

These verses are difficult to comprehend. First, the day of which the passage speaks will be a unique day—a day of neither bright sunlight nor darkness. Second, we do not know how long that day will be. Third, that day is known only to the Lord. Perhaps the day will go on for an indefinite period of time, for we are told that evening will not come at the time it is expected. Rather than attempt to say more about something we do not understand, let us simply note what the Scripture states.

> And it shall be, in that day, that living waters shall go out from Jerusalem; half of them toward the former sea, and half of them toward the hinder sea; in summer and in winter shall it be (14:8).

This verse implies that Jerusalem will become a unique watershed, not necessarily because water will flow from the city of the Lord, but because it will be "living waters." Jesus was declared to be "a well of water springing up into everlasting life" (Jn. 4:14). It will be interesting to see just how this will be fulfilled when we return with Christ at His Second Coming.

The waters are said to flow "half of them toward the former sea, and half of them toward the hinder sea" (14:8b). More accurately, this should read the *eastern sea* and the *western sea*. The eastern sea is the Dead Sea, and the western is the Mediterranean. To clearly indicate the adequacy of the water, it is said to flow in both summer and winter. The rains in Israel end in the spring and usually do not return again until the fall. The long dry period through the summer often causes problems for the nation. These problems will be eliminated in the

Millennium, when a sufficient supply of living waters will flow in every direction all year long.

The Promise of a Divine Ruler

And the LORD shall be king over all the earth; in that day shall there be one LORD, and His name one (14:9).

If there is any verse in this book that lays hold of the human heart, it is this one. The earth has long been gripped by sin, and because of it we have the curses and maladies afflicting humanity. But this verse declares that Jesus Christ will come to be King of kings and Lord of lords. Believing mankind has lived for many millennia in anticipation of that day. The day for which believers have prayed and of which poets have written finally will arrive.

At the end of the verse is an especially meaningful phrase, "and his name one." Mankind has accepted as gods almost everything imaginable. They have made gods of the sun, the moon, and idols of wood and stone. Others have made gods of materialism, power, sex, greed, and almost anything else that can be named. When Christ returns, the days of idolatry will finally be over. The world will focus on the true and living God, the sovereign Lord of all the earth.

Promise of Divine Changes

All the land shall be turned like the Arabah from Geba to Rimmon south of Jerusalem; and it shall be lifted up, and inhabited in its place, from Benjamin's gate unto the place of the first gate, unto the corner gate, and from the tower of Hananel unto the king's winepresses (14:10).

The earth must have gone through some tremendous geographic changes after the fall of Adam and Eve. For example, the location of the Garden of Eden can no longer be determined, although it certainly must have been a beautiful area, the center of life.

Jerusalem, as the royal city of this new King, will receive all it has longed for through the centuries. It will be the prominent and predominant city of the world. London, Washington, Paris, and other great cities will have lost their stature. Jerusalem's beauty will far surpass that of the earlier Garden of Eden, and its world stature will be greater than any city in history.

While the city of the King will be lifted up, the land around it will be flattened as a plain, so that the capital of the world can be seen from afar in every direction. The cities of Geba and Rimmon represent roughly the northern and southern boundaries of the portion of Israel given to the tribe of Judah. In that future day, regardless of the direction from which people approach Jerusalem, they will be able to see it lifted above all other cities in the land.

> And men shall dwell in it, and there shall be no more utter destruction; but Jerusalem shall be safely inhabited (14:11).

The name *Jerusalem* in the Hebrew means *city of peace*. Yet this city has probably known more war and bloodshed than any other city in the world. Located at the very navel of the earth, one empire after another has moved against or through it. That sorrowful condition will end when the Lord returns. Then it will experience no more destruction but only peace. It will no longer need walls and fortifications, and people will be able to live there without fear. It will truly be the city of peace when "the Prince of Peace" (Isa. 9:6) begins His reign. He will be its protection.

The Promise of Plagues to Her Enemies

> And this shall be the plague with which the LORD will smite all the peoples that have fought against Jerusalem: their flesh shall consume away while they stand upon their feet, and their eyes shall consume away in their holes, and their tongue shall consume away in their mouth (14:12).

The living enemies of Jerusalem will have to face the plagues of a righteous and just Lord. This verse graphically describes these plagues. As the enemies of the Lord stand on their feet, the soft parts of their bodies will be consumed. They will die a horrible death while simply standing in place.

The second plague that will befall the enemies of Jerusalem is described as a great tumult, amounting to total confusion. The Lord will bring such confusion on His enemies that they will turn on their own people.

138 ZECHARIAH

And Judah also shall fight at Jerusalem; and the wealth of all the nations round about shall be gathered together—gold, and silver, and apparel—in great abundance (14:14).

This passage also deals with the wealth of the nations. Israel will *take an offering* from the goods of the armies that oppose her. In the first verse of this chapter, the enemies of the Lord and of the Jews had defeated the city and were sitting in the midst of it counting the spoils. Now the spoils of the world will be literally dumped and abandoned in the middle of the city, to be gathered up by those who were earlier defeated.

And so shall be the plague of the horse, of the mule, of the camel, and of the ass, and of all the beasts that shall be in these tents, as this plague (14:15).

Finally, it is recorded that even the animals that served the heathen armies will be plagued. God will bring about a total spoiling of the would-be spoilers.

The Promise of Divine Worship

In the ancient world, various armies depended on their gods to bring them victory. When the battle was won, the victor laid claim to the spoils and humiliated the defeated army or people. One way of humiliating the enemy was to taunt him by saying, "My god is better than your god." If the conquered people wanted to stay alive, they had to worship the god of the victorious army.

It becomes apparent that the destruction of the people in the enemy armies will not be universal. Some of them will be allowed to live to fulfill the verses at the end of this book.

And it shall come to pass that every one that is left of all the nations which came against Jerusalem shall even go up from year to year to worship the King, the LORD of hosts, and to keep the feast of tabernacles (14:16).

The nations of the Millennium will be required to worship the King. They will make annual pilgrimages to Jerusalem to worship "the LORD of hosts.'' This is a military phrase used of the Lord of the armies. God will be acknowledged and worshiped by all who enter the Millennium.

Furthermore, the nations will keep the Feast of Tabernacles, also called the Feast of Booths. This is interesting, for of all the feasts of Israel, Tabernacles speaks most clearly of God coming to earth to dwell with mankind. This point is made in Matthew 17, when Jesus was transfigured before Peter, James, and John. In ignorance, they thought Jesus was on earth to stay, and they wanted to set up three booths. The idea is that God will tabernacle, or live, with mankind. The nations of the Millennium will be reminded every year that God is dwelling with mankind in the person of Jesus Christ, ruling and reigning from Jerusalem.

> And it shall be that whoever will not come up of all the families of the earth unto Jerusalem to worship the King, the LORD of hosts, even upon them shall be no rain. And if the family of Egypt go not up, and come not, that have no rain, there shall be the plague, with which the LORD will smite the nations that come not up to keep the feast of tabernacles (14:17-18).

Going to Jerusalem to worship will not be a matter of choice. People will have to go or face the consequence, which will be lack of rain resulting in a lack of crops.

Using Egypt as an illustration, the Scriptures point out that not only will there be no rain, but the plague previously mentioned will linger. It is clear that Jesus Christ will truly be Lord of the earth and will rule in absolute power.

> In that day shall there be upon the bells of the horses, HOLINESS UNTO THE LORD; and the pots in the LORD's house shall be like the bowls before the altar (14:20).

God is holy. Everything in the city of Jerusalem will point to His holiness. Bells on the horses will ring out constantly, ''HOLINESS UNTO THE LORD.'' Simple things like the pots in the Lord's house and all other houses will ring out the message of this truth. The concept is that because God is a holy God, holiness will be the way of life on the earth.

Finally, the writer says, ''and in that day there shall be no more a Canaanite in the house of the LORD of hosts'' (14:21b). The Canaanites represented idol worship, and such worship had even crept into the

Temple of the Lord (cp. ch. 8-11). When Jesus Christ establishes His kingdom, all idol worship will be removed. Only true worship will be practiced.

Conclusion

God has not forgotten Jerusalem, nor has He forgotten the Jewish people. The book penned by the Prophet Zechariah makes this truth exceedingly clear.

There will be both physical and spiritual deliverance for the nation and land of Abraham's children. At the beginning of this study we found a discouraged, disillusioned group of God's people huddled below their destroyed city. At the close we find a redeemed, victorious people living in a city that has been lifted up to become the capital of the world. The Messiah-King is reigning. Redeemed Jewry will have both physical and spiritual peace.

No, God has not forgotten His people—He never has and He never will. God remembers His people. It is joy inexpressible for us to belong to the King today. It is my prayer that you know Him as your Savior and Lord.

Bibliography

Baldwin, Joyce G. *Haggai, Zechariah, Malachi, Tyndale Old Testament Commentaries*. Downers Grove, Illinois: Inter Varsity Press, 1972.

Baron, David. *The Visions and Prophecies of Zechariah*. Grand Rapids, Michigan: Kregel Press, 1918, 1972.

Chisholm, Robert B., Jr. *Interpreting the Minor Prophets*. Grand Rapids, Michigan: Academie Books, Zondervan Publishing House, 1990.

Colón, Peter J. *Zechariah, A Historical and Prophetic Study on Israel and Jerusalem*. Unpublished, 1990.

Feinberg, Charles L. *The Minor Prophets*. Chicago, Illinois: Moody Press, 1948-1952.

Feinberg, Charles L. *God Remembers, A Study of Zechariah*. Portland, Oregon: Multonomah Press, 1965, 1979.

Hartman, Fred H. "Zechariah." In *Israel My Glory*. Bellmawr, New Jersey: The Friends of Israel Gospel Ministry, Inc., 1983-1984.

Kimichi, Rabbi David. *Commentary Upon the Prophecies of Zechariah*. Translated from the Hebrew by the Rev. A. M'Caul. London, England: James Duncan, 1837.

Luck, G. Coleman. *Zechariah, A Study of the Prophetic Visions of Zechariah*. Chicago, Illinois: Moody Press, 1957, 1969.

McGee, J. Vernon. "Zechariah," *Through the Bible Commentary Series*. Nashville, Tennessee: Thomas Nelson, 1975, 1991.

Meyer, F.B. *The Prophet of Hope, Studies in Zechariah*. Fort Washington, Pennsylvania: Christian Literature Crusade, 1952.

Saxe, Raymond Hyman. *Israel's Future Triumph, An Exposition of Zechariah 12-14*. Ann Arbor, Michigan: Grace Bible Publication, 1978.

Unger, Merrill F. *Zechariah: Prophet of Messiah's Glory.* Grand Rapids, Michigan: Zondervan Publishing House, 1963, 1976.

Unger, Merrill F. *Unger's Commentary on the Old Testament.* Chicago, Illinois: Moody Press, 1982.

Walvoord, John F., and Roy B. Zuck. *The Bible Knowledge Commentary.* Wheaton, Illinois: Victor Books, Division of Scripture Press Publications, 1987.